D0639379

READY
SET
SELL!

How To
TURN PROSPECTS INTO PAYCHECKS
AND LIVE A HAPPIER LIFE

JIM WRIGLEY

Market Share Sherpas
Nashville, TN
2015

First Edition: May 2015

ISBN #978-0-9963355-0-8

Library of Congress Control Number: 2015907567

1. Business & Money 2. Marketing & Sales 3. Sales & Selling
I. Wrigley, Jim II. Ready, Set, Sell

Project/Developmental Editor: Paul Bregande
Consultant Editor: Ellen Goldman Frasco
Cover/Book Design: David Bregande

Market Share Sherpas, LLC
2124 Golf Club Lane
Nashville, TN 37215

Ordering Information: Special discounts are available on quantity purchases by corporations, associations and others. For details, contact the publisher at the address listed above or by email at info@mssherpas.com. For orders by U.S. trade bookstores and wholesalers, visit www.ingramcontent.com

Printed in the United States of America

In memory of my Dad,
whose insights and career path
strongly influenced my own.

Acknowledgements

I would like to offer special thanks to the following individuals, each of whom provided valuable assistance toward the completion of this book:

Kathryn Beckman, whose contribution not only resulted in a better product, but whose question, "Why write a manuscript, if you aren't going to publish it?" led me to commit fully to the process;

Paul Bregande, for organizing my concepts, making my writing digestible, and doing all (and I do mean all) the hard work that was required to bring this project to fruition;

David Bregande, for the exceptional cover and book design, which will make it stand out on a crowded shelf, and facilitate a great reading experience;

Ellen Goldman Frasco, for providing the editorial finishing touch, and for not laughing at me when I asked, "Can I have the final version by next week?"

Those who reviewed the manuscript prior to its publication, including Leslie Whitehead, Nick Dantona, and my mother, Carol Wrigley, who is still sending me suggestions;

And finally, my sales team members, who attempted, challenged, adjusted, and ultimately mastered the tactics and techniques in this book with outstanding success.

Table of Contents

Foreword

I first met Jim Wrigley in Nashville, Tennessee in 1995. He was the Senior Vice President of Sales for a small, but growing financial services firm that would later become one of the fastest growing privately held companies in the United States. He had just hired me for an outside sales position, which meant that we would be spending some quality one-on-one time together.

Training at that time was like drinking from a fire hose and I learned many valuable tactics and techniques, which Jim promised would not only give me an advantage over the competition in business, but would improve nearly every relationship in life. I remember being somewhat skeptical, and perhaps even taken aback by his enthusiasm for all that he thought possible, but I listened carefully nonetheless. Today, I'm glad that I did, for I clearly see that he was spot on with that notion.

To this day I continue to employ Jim's advice on a daily

basis in my executive roles and regularly pass on his wisdom to others. In short, he treats each interaction in life as an opportunity, and turns each day in the field into an exciting problem-solving adventure. Best of all, as I have witnessed, he generates extraordinary results.

I am pleased, that now others will also have the opportunity to learn how and why Jim's system of selling works. It is with pleasure that I encourage you to spend the time to learn how to become a more effective, more financially successful salesperson, and enjoy life to a greater extent.

To greater results,

Clint Carnell
Chief Executive, Perseon Corporation
Board member, CEO and serial entrepreneur

"Nothing Happens Until Somebody Sells Something."

-Thomas J. Watson

Preface

"You should write a book." I've heard that phrase multiple times, usually after a winning sales call or a strategic discussion about how to close a new account. But despite having a notebook filled with source material, I never took the suggestion very seriously until one memorable day in March of 2006. It happened on of all places, an airplane.

The CEO of a California-based ergonomic furniture company sat awkwardly in the dreaded middle seat of Row 16 on our flight from Nashville to San Francisco. To say his legs were long would be an understatement - they were Abraham Lincoln long. As I sat comfortably in my aisle seat, he looked to me like an NBA forward sitting on a child's tricycle. Judging by the look on his face, my guess was that he felt that way, too.

I had a feeling that he, like most travelers, didn't want to talk. He probably just wanted to read or rest. Truth be told, I hadn't really felt like chatting either, which is ironic given that I make my living endorsing the benefits of speaking up.

But I knew that we both had four hours before we landed in San Francisco, and since we were sitting next to each other, I decided to initiate a brief conversation.

"Before I spill my coffee on you, I thought I would introduce myself," I said, intending for nothing more than a minute of friendly banter. "I'm Jim."

"Pleasure to meet you Jim," he replied. "I'm Todd and I accept your apology in advance, with the sincere hope it doesn't come to that."

As he spoke, I'm sure he didn't realize that this brief exchange would lead him - just a few weeks later - to pay me $25,000 for my expertise. For that matter, I didn't know that it would also be the impetus for me to begin writing this book. With the ice now broken, we both settled in for the flight and before the plane had even reached the runway, Todd posed the $25,000 question.

"So, what do you do?" he asked.

"That's a great question," I replied. "You know how just about everybody in business wants to make more money?"

"Ha, more than most," Todd shot back.

"Well, I teach people how to do just that." I said, still unaware of what he did for a living.

"Really? And how do you do that?" he asked in a friendly tone, but with a noticeable air of disbelief. This was exactly what I was expecting to hear.

"Well," I said, "Depending on what you do, I could probably teach you too." With that, the sales process had begun.

Like every person I have met in my career, Todd was either

going to be a prospect, a referral source for my business, or at the least, a new acquaintance. After telling me that he was the CEO of an ergonomics furniture company, he posed my favorite follow-up question to hear.

"How do you do that?" He said, inviting me to offer him my value proposition. So that's exactly what I did.

First, I shared a brief story about a previous client whose business had gained a twenty percent increase in market share after I had conducted a training session on the importance of developing an effective, repeatable sales process. Then, I described the key elements of my proven strategy for helping individuals and organizations reach their desired reasonable revenue goal. Finally, I bet Todd that I would be able to make a similar impact on his company's sales results by providing just one day of coaching.

Todd agreed that his team could use some additional training, but didn't believe that great selling techniques could be learned in a single day.

"My experience has been that selling techniques that really work take a long time to learn," he stated. "And unfortunately, time is not on my side."

"Todd," I replied, "what I have to offer is truly unique and will enable your salespeople to generate predictable outcomes. Now may not be the time, but if you're serious about improving your results, we should absolutely talk further at another time."

As I had intended, Todd was intrigued enough to continue the conversation and invited me to call him the following week. Mission accomplished.

On the follow-up phone call with Todd, I reinforced the value my sales strategies would bring to his organization. And after just twenty minutes, having satisfactorily addressed all of his questions, we agreed to a no-risk, open-ended agreement, following through on my initial bet.

By the terms that I had proposed, I would make a two-hour presentation at Todd's national sales meeting and afterward, after his team got to try out what I was suggesting, he would pay me whatever he felt it was worth. I was happy to take my chances, knowing that my sales methodology was beyond price, having generated such successful results for my previous clients. After Todd had attended my presentation, and excitingly shared that they indeed had landed a key new account, he willingly offered me $25,000 as my compensation. As it turned out, I made a pretty good bet that day, and Todd remains a valued client and vocal advocate of my services.

In doing so, I reinforced a valuable lesson on that flight that I learned long ago and continue to advocate to all who will listen. I had seized an opportunity to speak up when I could have chosen to read, listen to music or say nothing at all. By simply executing a repeatable sales process that I developed long before this casual interaction, I was able to secure my desired outcome and more importantly, help a business exceed its revenue goals. The lesson: Deals always close when both parties win, and you'll get nothing if you don't take a shot.

And as a further, longer-term result, that company's CEO convinced me that I should write this book.

Introduction

If I were to tell you that in just one day, you could acquire some new selling skills and make a few adjustments to your selling strategy that could launch you to the top of your profession, would you be ready and willing to take the time to learn them? I'm referring to tactics and techniques – some tried and true, and some entirely new – that could help you achieve the following:

Exceed your sales objectives

Increase your income

Achieve Salesperson of the Year

Earn the respect of your peers

Live a happier life

As a coach, I often pose this somewhat rhetorical question as a manner of opening my sales training seminars. Participants invariably respond enthusiastically in the affirmative; but they also find it hard to believe that anything that could make such a meaningful, positive impact on their success may be learned in a single day. Fortunately, I have always relished the opportunity to turn doubters into believers. I am proud to state that many of these salespeople, having adopted and employed my proven strategies, are today among my most vocal endorsers.

When I decided to write this book, I deliberately sought to replicate the format of my live seminars, by providing readers with valuable information that could be easily digested in just one day's worth of reading. As such, don't expect any "deep dives" into complicated selling theories. As salespeople, most of us don't have time for that. Do expect to learn relevant, relatable, and repeatable processes that absolutely work, often on the very first try. With practice and disciplined execution, your reward will be greater success in business and in life.

Keep in mind as you read through the material, that although my role today is that of a coach or a teacher, I am first and foremost a salesperson just like you. Despite having held senior-level sales management positions, I have always made my living the same way as you do. I have worn the same blue suit, white shirt, red tie and polished black shoes with pre-maturely worn soles. I understand the daily hardships all salespeople face in the field. I have missed the connecting flights, and have sat in the reception area for hours only to hear my prospect's assistant say, "Mr. Decision Maker *won't* see you now." My nose and my knuckles, like yours, have been metaphorically bloodied while participating in the often grueling, but always exciting profession of sales.

Challenges notwithstanding, I have learned that "whatever the mind can conceive and believe, it can achieve." I first came upon this quote in Napoleon Hill's book, *Think and Grow Rich*, and have referred to it often throughout my career. Today, with more than twenty years of positive results and countless testimonials from happy customers, I feel strongly that what I have to share with you is of tremendous value. Should you follow the path ahead, I am confident that you will be able to overcome objections more effectively and master a winning sales process that will bring you greater results, day in and day out.

Isn't That Your Truck?

My sales career began at the age of nineteen, when I landed a position as a route salesperson at the 7-Up Bottling Corporation's Norwalk, Connecticut distribution facility. Although some would not consider driving a delivery truck to be a traditional sales job, I can assure you that it was. My compensation was 100% commission-based, and "selling" was the only way that I made money.

At the beginning of each day, I would load a mix of products on to my truck, and would be responsible for selling and delivering as many cases of soda as possible. Since I had a PhD in sales (meaning that I was poor, hungry and driven), I would load my truck each morning to its maximum capacity of 600 cases. My sales commission was $.65 per case, so to make the most money; I went out fully *expecting* to sell out the truck.

From this job, I learned two valuable, lifelong selling lessons. The first was how to hustle. In the soda delivery business, you didn't have to be a great salesperson in order to make a decent wage. You simply had to hustle. And because there were only so many hours in a day, hustling as quickly as possible allowed you to see more customers and usually earn more money. The second lesson, one that I learned the hard way by hustling too much, was that it is not always a good idea to take shortcuts.

As it happened, several of my sales stops included corner liquor stores located in neighborhoods with some of the highest crime rates in the state. As such, I was required to lock every door on the truck at all times in order to eliminate the risk of losing inventory. Even still, it was not uncommon for cases of soda to suddenly "disappear." In fact, my handcart was once stolen off the back of my truck at a red light, only to be sold back to me as a "slightly used" one for fifty dollars just a few blocks away.

One day, I decided to buck procedure and devise a shortcut that I was convinced would increase my speed of delivery. I locked the doors as usual, but then left the key in the lock to avoid the need to dig it out of my pocket when I returned. For a while, my shortcut worked and as a hustler, I was pleased. That is, until one time when an enterprising soul guessed correctly that the key to the truck's ignition might also be dangling from that same lock. I never saw the new owner of my truck get in, but it wasn't long before he was driving away without me. As I stood inside the corner store dumbfounded, the storeowner pointed out the window and asked me a most obvious question. He said, "Hey, Jim...isn't that your truck?"

I certainly didn't earn big money as a salesperson that day. What I did learn is that not every short cut, cuts things short. Prior to the incident, because of my youth, everyone in the warehouse called me "the kid." After, my supervisor decided to give me a new nickname, one that has endured to this day. I am now known as, "the kid who lost the truck."

The Journey to Percentage-Wise Improvement

I would not recommend beginning your sales career by losing a $75,000 truck; there is a substantially less expensive way to learn the lessons you will need to achieve a "percentage-wise improvement" in your results. I use this term because in sales, a slight advantage is all we really need to win. You might not think that achieving a "percentage-wise improvement" (that could come from the simple effort of hustling) would be enough to satisfy your expectations, but often times, the smallest of margins can make the difference between winning and losing.

Horses win races by a nose. Golfers win tournaments by a stroke. In many competitions, the difference between first and second place is a gold versus a silver medal. In all of these cases, there is a dramatic difference between the prize money and adulation that comes from winning or from finishing in second place, if only a fraction of measurement behind. And therein lies the good news. Oftentimes winning means we only need to be just slightly better than the competition. And thus, here you will find a digest of little things that will go a long way to create that slim margin, causing you to win more deals that you might previously have imagined.

What Lies Ahead

On my own quest to seek improvement, I have always found it tremendously helpful to keep in mind that as salespeople, we only have control over three things:

Our attitude

The quantity of our sales calls

The quality of our sales calls

Everything else is out of our control. The economy may fluctuate, the competition may cut prices, our territory may be reduced in size, and the shipping department may botch our order. You name it and it may happen – and often it does. But setbacks don't keep successful people from succeeding.

Sometimes the most difficult part of any journey toward improvement is how to get started. Conveniently I have found that even just a single word may be all the incentive you need to get moving. In Part One of this book, we will lay the foundation for your selling success by discussing how decisions are made; exploring the best ways to get people's attention; and providing insights into how to build a winning culture for yourself, which will help you stand out as a recognized winner in any organization. And we will distill that down into a single word as a simple reminder to keep us moving.

Parts Two through Five have been purposely organized into Acts rather than Chapters, to encourage salespeople like you, to take specific ACT-ions in order to gain an advantage over the competition and improve your selling results. In Part Two, we will cover the importance of having the right attitude. The discussion of Acts 1 through 10 will include examining how we talk; how we think; how we carry ourselves; and how we behave - all of which have an enormous impact on our success.

In Part Three, which features Acts 11 through 17, we will confront call quantity issues. This is the area in which old-fashioned hard work comes into play. If you know that it takes hearing "no" ten times to get one "yes," then you must know the quickest way to get nine people to say it.

When you arrive at Part Four, the discussion of Acts 18 through 27, we will focus on the topic of the quality of your calls. You will learn how to turn presentations into conversations; discover the importance of building a repeatable process; and learn how embracing even the toughest objections may cause them to melt away. We'll also discuss how to use the power of speaking from experience to command the attention and respect of others, as well as learn how to shorten the sales cycle with an approach that will result in prospects following your recommendations.

Finally, in Part Five, featuring Acts 28 and 29, we will help you to determine where your skills fit most effectively into a sales organization. Are you best suited to be a hunter of new business; a farmer of existing relationships; a combination of both; or someone completely different? Since we know that it's impossible to fit a square peg into a round hole, you will be encouraged to examine your personal strengths in order to discover your ideal role.

By the end of the book, you will be equipped with a new set of skills, and at that point, we will all be speaking the same language - the language of success! Since one day is all that is required to learn how to sell more effectively, make today the day to get ready, get set, and begin winning all the deals you desire.

Part One

Building the Foundation

How Decisions are Made

In its most simple form, your job as a salesperson is to identify people who need your products or services and persuade them to buy. In his book, *Just Listen*, author Mark Goulston introduced *The Persuasion Cycle*, as an approach that he has used during his career as a psychiatrist, business consultant and hostage negotiation trainer to help him deal with difficult people in all kinds of scenarios.

The Persuasion Cycle - by Mark Goulston

1. From **resisting** to **listening**
2. From **listening** to **considering**
3. From **considering** to **willing to do**
4. From **willing to do** to **doing**
5. From **doing** to **glad they did**
6. From **glad they did** to **continuing to do**

When I was reading Goulston's book, it occurred to me that this approach could also be applied to the business of selling - to help determine where prospects are in the decision-making process - and then to help them as to what to do next to move them toward a final transaction. But to make the cycle even more useful, I decided to add another step to this approach to account for the new business we seek to be generated from referrals received after the sale.

The Referral Step - by Jim Wrigley

7. To **telling everyone else what they are doing!**

For the purpose of this book, I will refer to the entire cycle, which includes my final step, as *The Sales Decision Chain.* When coaching salespeople, I compare this cycle to a roadmap that we should always refer back to so that we can ensure that we never get lost in the sales process. If we know, "Where we are now" and can verbalize, "What we see," we can usually make the directional adjustments needed or get help if necessary, to reach our destination.

I have often met individual sales contributors, and even entire sales teams who have told me that they are feeling lost in terms of succeeding at their objectives. It is indeed frustrating when you feel stuck in the sales process or have failed, or are actively failing, to meet your objectives. When I ask salespeople why they think that this has occurred, they usually respond by saying they just, "Don't know." At that point, it is not unusual to find out that the real problem has been that they have not been working from any sort of strategic sales plan and have therefore not been in control over their own destinies.

Selling is a simple process of using repeatable processes to move your prospects through their decision chain and winning together by taking incremental baby steps along the way. Are your prospects **resisting?** If so, then per the sales chain you must understand why they are **resisting** before you can get them to **listen.** In the preface of the book, I relayed my story about meeting the CEO of a furniture company and earning his business. You might remember that in that situation it was only when my prospect was **listening** that I was able to take him to the next step of **considering** the possibility of engaging my services. That CEO is now at Step 7, i.e. **telling everyone else what he's doing** and serving as an excellent reference for my services.

Unfortunately, many salespeople and organizations are so happy to earn a commission check or bonus for getting their prospect from **willing to do** to actually **doing** (and often without a plan to even get that far) that they forget that the real money - the recurring dollars, referrals to other new prospects and add-on sales – may be found between Step 4 and my Step 7, the points at which the customer becomes a promoter of your products and services.

Take a second look at the back end of The Sales Decision Chain:

4. From **willing to do** to **doing**

5. From **doing** to **glad they did**

6. From **glad they did** to **continuing to do**

7. To **telling everyone else what they are doing!**

At Step 7, your customer is so satisfied and enthused by the sales experience that he or she will actually sell your products for you. Have you ever attended a film that was so good that you told your friends that they had to go see it? This is Step 7 in action and if enough people have also told their friends about that "must see" film, it will eventually become a block-buster hit.

Take it from the coach: Selling is far more exciting and exponentially more rewarding when you can predict outcomes and calculate winning percentages. Utilizing the Sales Decision Chain will help you accomplish both of those tasks, but first you need to learn how to get other people's attention.

Getting Other People's Attention

If you are going to become a professional persuader, you will need to master the art of getting other people's attention. The quickest way to take prospects from **resisting** to **listening** is to employ three simple techniques from an age-old practice known as the Socratic Method.

In short, the Socratic Method is a form of discussion between individuals that is based on asking questions in order to stimulate critical thinking in others. This method works because it fosters self-discovery and produces moments when a person embraces an idea you placed into the discussion, as his or her own. Once your prospects start talking and want to be heard, you will know that you have their full attention. Since they have become engaged in the conversation (as talkers) and are no longer **resisting,** the chance that they will start **listening** (when it's your turn to talk) improves dramatically.

Following a practice that I believe Socrates would surely endorse, I start each of my sales conversations with a short story that contains a message related to the relevant subject matter. At the conclusion of the story, I engage my prospect by *asking him or her for feedback on the story.*

If I had just spoken about my new car's incredible gas mileage or the amazing round of golf I had shot last week, it would be more than likely that my prospect would follow up with a related personal anecdote (talking), and as a result, this keeps the conversation moving.

Once *the prospect* starts talking, it's *my turn* to start listening and to display genuine interest in whatever it is that he or she had chosen to share. If the prospect feels that I am seeking to understand his or her point of view, the prospect will offer me the same courtesy in return. The result will be an open dialogue that will increase the likelihood of the prospect listening to the rest of the sales conversation. In essence, this technique helps to create an environment that is conducive to solving problems.

Another lesson I have learned from employing the Socratic Method is that in order to be an effective communicator, it is important to "keep it simple." No matter how complicated the product or service, I have always strived to conduct my selling efforts at the eighth grade level. Breaking down the description of my product's key features into easily digestible snippets makes it easier for other people to understand its utility.

Salespeople often become frustrated when prospects resist their ideas. To take prospects from **resisting** to **listening** and on to **considering** your solutions, you need to practice and employ three simple techniques derived from the Socratic

Method: 1) Tell engaging short stories and ask for feedback; 2) Listen with genuine interest to encourage mutually-empathetic discussions, and; 3) Always keep it simple. Remember that in sales, mapping out your route and executing a well-planned course of action are the most efficient ways to reach your desired destination.

Defining Your Selling Culture

I'm confident that you would agree that establishing a sales culture that is embraced by every member of a team is critical to a company's success. In order to define that specific sales culture, a manual that "speaks" a company's language, promotes the desired culture, and enables self-discovery is often created at larger organizations. But for the smaller clients I have worked with, or even larger ones, without a set sales methodology, this book can serve as a de-facto manual that may be utilized by any sales team.

Word Choice Matters

Time and again, I have seen how the power of the written word could be used to help develop a focused and committed team of professionals. To illustrate my point, consider a well-known phrase that has been associated with the United States Postal Service - one that is as relevant today as it was when it was penned over one hundred years ago. The words of the phrase convey a single-minded approach that is used by the entire organization and seeks to set the standard by which the employees of the agency should conduct business every day of the year.

> *"And neither snow, nor rain, nor heat, nor gloom of night, nor the winds of change, nor a nation challenged, will stay us from the swift completion of our appointed rounds. Ever."*

After all of these years, it's hard for us not to equate that saying with the United States Postal Service, since it has become the unofficial doctrine that serves as the basis for its highly disciplined culture. What if individual post office branches did not actively adhere to this doctrine? How would the mail delivery process be affected? What if the folks in blue and grey only delivered the mail when it was convenient; when they weren't too busy; or when they didn't have internal meetings to attend? What would be the outcome?

My favorite part of the creed is the last sentence, which contains just a single word. "Ever" reminds employees that they must do their part to get the job done, regardless of what it takes to meet that goal. It implies that without their individual efforts, the operation will falter. With that one word, they are aware of what is required to be successful.

The existence of a common culture will make the difference between mediocrity and excellence. So what is your company's creed?

If It's to Be, It's Up to Me

I had decided long ago that my success would not be defined by the success of the organization for which I worked. A job, as great as it might be, should not define who we are as individuals. It is our duty to create our own definition of who we are and then be the very best that we could be.

By developing your own creed, defining and achieving your own goals, and then lending your specific talents to an organization, you could significantly increase your value to the organization and also stand out as a valued contributor. As you begin to think of your success as an individual, rather than as a part of an organization, you will sense the control of your own destiny shifting toward you and away from territory cuts, compensation plan changes, the revolving door of senior management, and a myriad of other worrisome events that are out of your control. As long as you are in charge of you, you are going to come up a winner.

Just one word, like "ever" in the United States Postal Service creed, could carry a powerful message. My word is "WIN," but not for the obvious reason. Although I certainly like to win and enjoy all the rewards that are associated with winning, I'm actually more motivated by *not losing*. For me, losing means that someone else got the deal or reward that should have gone to me and/or to my team.

WIN is an acronym for the question "What's Important Now?" Since 1988, when I first heard that acronym used by legendary football coach Lou Holtz, I have incorporated the concept of WIN into every sales training I have conducted. According to Holtz, he had instructed his players to ask themselves "What's Important Now?" as they went through each day, in order to learn to focus on what mattered most at any given time. His simple lesson was that in the face of an overwhelming number of choices we encounter on a daily basis, this one powerful question helps us to prioritize our actions and decision-making. Obviously, Coach Holtz understood that our choices have a lasting impact on our personal and professional lives and that making the right choices helps to put us on the clearest path to achieving excellence.

For me, WIN is both a question and a statement that has impacted both my present and my future. By always focusing on What's Important Now, I ensure that my energy is being invested in the right things at the right time, e.g. completing my weekly expense reports in a timely fashion in order to prevent a year-end accounting nightmare. WIN is my personal one-word mission statement that impels me to move forward.

Finding Your Word

Now it's your turn to find your word. Since this book is all about taking ACT-ion, let's warm up with a simple exercise. Reflect on the only three areas that you as a salesperson could control to impact your paycheck and your personal happiness: Your attitude; the quantity of your calls; and the quality of your calls. Next, write down as many words that come to mind to describe the person that you aspire to become. **Ready?**

As it relates to attitude, you might consider words like:
Positive • Confident • Decisive • Delighted • Grateful

If call quantity is the area on which you would like to focus, you might consider words like:
Dedicated • Disciplined • Productive • Motivated • Consistent

Examples of words related to the quality of what you say during your sales conversations might be:
Enthusiastic • Memorable • Polished • Helpful • Exceptional

Set? From your list, pick the only word that is most likely to remind you of the person you want to become. So what word did you choose?

Sell! Now tape your word next to the trackpad on your computer; write it in soap on your bathroom mirror; print it on a sticky note and tape it onto the dashboard of your car. Perhaps an even better idea would be to take a new kind of "selfie," e.g. take a picture of your word with your mobile device and make it your wallpaper so that you'll see it all day long. If you would like to share your word with someone else, do it, since it is always a good idea to have another person hold you accountable for keeping your word. Expect these daily reminders of your mission to have a powerful, positive impact on your state of mind as well as to set you on the path toward achieving the percentage-wise improvement you need to surpass the competition.

Part Two

Controlling Your Attitude

*I have always felt strongly that the bulk of the income we earn as salespeople is directly related to our degree of mental focus. Some of the best coaching advice I have ever received was that I should 'use my head, but move my feet.' In order to get your prospects to move their feet - from **considering** to **willing to do** and then from **willing to do** to **doing** - you must approach them with the proper attitude. Part 2 explores non-verbal and verbal techniques that may be used to positively impact the way you are perceived by others and also to accelerate your sales results.*

Act 1

The Meaning of Commitment

We have just discussed the importance of identifying one word that could serve as your personal daily mission statement, i.e. a consistent reminder of where you want to be or the person you want to become. Here's a word you might have chosen: Committed.

To succeed in sales as well as in life, one must carefully construct a plan of attack that leverages the knowledge accrued through experience and then applies it using a disciplined and recurring approach. In more simple terms, achieving success in sales (without reliance on luck) is a matter of doing the right things at the right times with the right people, and should be orchestrated by a fully committed leader who is responsible for the entire process. I could not imagine any buyer who would be willing to move through Step 3 (from **consid-**

ering to **willing to do**) or Step 4 (from **willing to do** to **doing**) of The Sales Decision Chain if his or her salesperson did not outwardly demonstrate that he or she was fully committed to the success of the project.

Most of us think that our level of commitment is already satisfactory, as if somehow that's a given. We fully believe that we are "all-in" when it comes to our job and we even resent the mere suggestion that we are not. But if we were to be honest with ourselves, we might admit that we are not always as committed as we should be, and could always do better.

Personally, I have always found it fascinating that Tiger Woods, one of the greatest golfers of all time, uses a coach. Even with multiple championship trophies on his shelf, his consistent work ethic is extraordinary. Regardless of his level of success, and even in the face of highly publicized personal and professional failures, he seems to continually strive to get better. I believe there is great value in trying to understand what makes him tick.

Although I have heard people say that Tiger Woods is a "natural," I am certain that he would disagree with that assessment. He embodies a philosophy that many of us often forget - that practice makes perfect. And when he practices, he does so with the same intensity, determination and focus that he brings to Sunday at the Masters. It is obvious to me that Tiger Woods understands that it takes more than talent to achieve excellence. His unwavering commitment and disciplined approach to the game have been what keeps him ahead of the competition.

The Commitment Test

You are the only person who could honestly say if you are committed to your job. You may *say* you are 100 percent committed and might even believe it, but your actions will always speak louder than your words. Here is an ACT-ion to help you determine whether you're "all-in" or have one foot out the door.

1. Take a look at your assigned sales objectives.

2. How do you feel about them?

3. With your answer in mind, set a sales number to which you will commit to achieve over the next ninety days.

The Results are In

Did you choose a lower or higher number than your current assigned sales objective? If you picked a number that was lower than the objective assigned by your employer, you are not as committed as you need to be. Do you lack confidence in the product or service you're selling (an attitude issue); or are you not seeing enough prospects (a quantity issue); or are you not saying the right things when you see those prospects (a quality issue)? Whatever the reason, it is clear that you are only "sort of" committed and unlike Tiger Woods, probably not going to win any championships or set any records anytime soon. But this is not the time to worry. Instead, consider this your time to work toward a "percentage-wise improvement" in one of the three areas you can control, so that the next time you are asked to do this exercise, you will be able to set a higher goal for yourself.

If you chose a higher number than what is expected of your organization, then it is clear that you are "all-in." When you are in alignment with your organization, you have the best opportunity to be the salesperson that stands above the rest. You should also keep in mind that sales objectives assigned by all companies are deliberately set high, and that good salespeople know that this is standard procedure.

There are really only two kinds of salespeople in this world - those who find an excuse and those who find a way. Salespeople who are 100 percent committed never make excuses; always set goals that are in line with their organization's expectations; and always find a way to be among the top performers. There is no value in daydreaming about better results, for this will only distract you from real achievement. To succeed, you must do one thing and that is to commit to your own, absolute success.

Act 2

Establishing a "Try It" Mentality

Salespeople fear nothing more than the outright rejection of their products and services, or in other words, hearing the dreaded word "no." For some, the fear of rejection may be so overwhelming that they talk themselves out of even calling on prospects because they are convinced that they already know the outcome. In truth, the fear of "no" is a terrible reason to avoid a potential sales conversation.

In my coaching, I encourage salespeople to establish a "try it" mentality that makes "no" irrelevant. Who cares if "no" is the answer? All that matters is that you had approached your prospect, which is far better than never having approached him or her at all. Since the sales process begins in earnest after receiving your first rejection, your most urgent task is to go out and get your "no" now.

Go Get Your "No"

If your "no" were a white tiger lurking in the jungles of the Amazon, would you be willing to go and find it? Unless you're Tarzan, your answer would likely be "probably not." But you would not be alone in feeling this way. In fact, most salespeople are hesitant to venture into unfamiliar territory, largely due to the fear of an uncertain or perhaps undesirable outcome. For them, it's easier to simply write off the task as impossible and move on to one that may be a bit more predictable. But what if that white tiger were sleeping in a locked cage and all you had to do to get there would be to follow a freshly paved trail? How would you have known that it would have been that easy if you weren't willing to venture into the jungle in the first place?

In sales, fear of the unknown is quite common and results in something known as "call reluctance." Even experienced sales veterans suffer from the anguish of having to knock again and again on an ice-cold door, since they have convinced themselves that there would be a "no" on the other side. But ironically, getting that "no" would be exactly what would be needed to get the sales process in motion.

By establishing a "try it" mentality - being willing to try anything and everything without the fear of an undesirable outcome - getting your "no" will be a snap. It could be as easy as approaching a prospect you have been reluctant to meet (perhaps because you have feared that he or she would not want to talk to you) and simply asking if he or she has heard of your products. When you get your "no," which is all you needed (and were in fact seeking) to get the conversation started, you would likely discover that the prospect would want to hear more about your proposed solution to his or her problem.

Facing Your Fear

Once during a training session, I wrote the word FEAR on a white board and then asked the group if they knew the meaning of the letters. Without hesitation, one rep said "Forget Everything And Run!" Although this was a highly creative response, and potentially effective if the white tiger you were seeking had not been locked in a cage, I had been seeking the response, "False Evidence Appearing Real."

My meaning of FEAR is one that I have tried to remember in the dark of the night when I have heard a sound that had suggested someone might have been in my house. Although in those situations, my heart is usually pounding and telling me to expect the worst, FEAR helps me take decisive action to discover the source, which invariably turns out to be the howling wind or the hum of the air conditioner. But in sales, the fear of making calls results in inaction, which in turn, may cause an entirely different level of anxiety.

I Didn't Say a Word

While I have sometimes feared the dark of night, I have

always thought I feared no one when it came to selling. That is, until six years ago when I found myself seated three feet away from Bill and Melinda Gates at a trendy Hawaiian restaurant. I hadn't been in Hawaii on business. I was actually on vacation and had figured that they were, too. But even knowing that I was not at a business meeting, I was still unable to say anything to them at all. Not a single word, not a single joke. I had been so intimidated by their presence that I hadn't even cracked a smile or looked their way. My usual amiable and chatty personality was nowhere to be found, since I had managed to convince myself that Bill and Melinda Gates would never talk to me under any circumstances. Afterwards, I replayed that scenario in my mind and thought about my reaction. I realized that I had just experienced full-on call reluctance. I had essentially talked myself out of talking, based purely on an irrational fear of rejection.

Looking back on that day (with regret, I might add), I keep thinking about how cool it would have been to talk shop with Bill Gates. Or if I were to take my imagination to the next level, to have actually sold him something or just as exciting, to have received a referral from him! In my mind, I kept thinking about an imaginary sales call that began with "Hello, this is Jim from XYZ Corp. I was talking with Bill Gates over breakfast in Hawaii and he suggested that I reach out to you." But unfortunately for me, I won't be making that call unless by some twist of fate, I happen to have the opportunity to be seated next to him again.

Ironically, I would have been happier sharing a story that

featured Bill Gates telling me to get lost rather than the one I have just shared with you. During the time when I should have been employing a "try it" strategy, I was instead paralyzed by fear. Since that day, my personal selling notes have contained the words, "What you fear is what you get," which reminds me that the desire for success must always be greater than the fear of failure.

Take ACT-ion

Before you dismiss the notion that call reluctance does not apply to you, here is this Act's ACT-ion. First, create a list of prospects that you would love to have as customers, but have either avoided or found impossible to reach. Next, describe the specific fear that has been preventing you from seeing each of them. Salespeople often justify their hesitancy by using such phrases as, "They're too big, too busy, or too important," or even something as silly-sounding as "they won't like me." But this doubting inner voice must be replaced with a "try it" mentality.

Now that you have your list, promise yourself that you will take a new course of action with each prospect, even if you are convinced that whatever you do is going to result in receiving a "no."

"Inaction breeds doubt and fear. Action breeds confidence and courage. If you want to conquer fear, do not sit home and think about it. Go out and get busy."

– Dale Carnegie

I have compared this simple exercise to cleaning a dirty window. Once you have the glass cleaner in hand, you find that it's very difficult to clean just one window. Most people end up cleaning every window in their home. Similarly, writing down your selling worries is your first step toward overcoming obstacles, one at a time, and achieving real sales momentum.

Act 3

Using Body Language
to Attract Business

What is the biggest problem you face when attempting to communicate your sales message to prospects? Are gatekeepers blocking your path? Are you speaking with people who are not decision makers? Is the decline in phone communication and the rise in email communication slowing you down? Are you being affected by limitations created by the required brevity of text messages? Each of these problems present legitimate communication challenges, but even when you do get to communicate with your prospect it should be noted that:

Words by themselves account for only
7 percent of your messaging.

That's right, only 7 percent. The other 93 percent of your communication is conveyed through non-verbal communications, e.g. body language; tone of voice; and even the use of emoticons and other symbols found in email and texting. As a result, arranging face-to-face meetings with your prospects provides you with the best chance of achieving sales success, followed by the use of messaging by VOIP communication (e.g. Skype™) and traditional phone dialogue. In the case of communicating by phone, a situation in which body language would seemingly not come into play; it is still critical that you maintain a proper outward physical stance. Even if your prospect cannot see you, he or she may still sense your general demeanor. Some inside salespeople who rely exclusively on the telephone, place a mirror in their offices in order to assess and improve their body language to project the proper attitude in their verbal communications. It is important to avoid projecting any semblance of self-consciousness or insecurity that would suggest that you are subordinate to your prospect, or you risk stalling the sales process.

Recently, I visited my local home improvement center with an interior designer whom I had hired to decorate my home. We were not in agreement about her paint color choices and I had no problem expressing my resistance. But she would not fold. Her sales job (which by the way, I was paying her to do) was to push me to places that I would never go on my own. She had the confidence to challenge me (her customer), referring to my preferred color choice as "little boy" blue versus what she had insisted was a better designer color.

Ultimately, I went with my designer's choice and the finished product ended up looking amazing. She had been able to convince me not just with her words, but also by her unwavering promise (commitment) that she had my best interests at heart. She had not feared her customer and had stood strong in the face of an obstacle, which in that situation happened to have been me. In the end, she got what she felt was best for me and we had both won.

> "Watch your thoughts, for they become words;
> Watch your words, for they become actions;
> Watch your actions, for they become habits;
> Watch your habits, for they become character;
> Watch your character, for it becomes your destiny."
>
> - Anonymous

Your Attitude Determines Your Altitude

When I coach sales teams, I ask everyone to begin with the assumption that our destiny is attaining a greater level of success than we have even imagined. I find it important to write down what that world looks like and then I believe that in order to get there we must have the right attitude about what it will take to get there. In fact, I felt it was so important that I took a minute to look up the proper definition of the word.

Attitude [**at**-i-tood, -tyood] *noun*

1. A settled way of thinking or feeling about someone or something, typically one that is reflected in a person's behavior: She took a tough attitude toward other people's indulgences | being competitive is an attitude of mind | differences in attitude were apparent between ethnic groups.

2. A position of the body proper to or implying an action or mental state: The boy was standing in an attitude of despair, his chin sunk on his chest.

3. Informal truculent or uncooperative behavior; a resentful or antagonistic manner: I asked the waiter for a clean fork, and all I got was attitude.

4. Informal individuality and self-confidence as manifested by behavior or appearance; style: She snapped her fingers with attitude.

5. The orientation of an aircraft or spacecraft, relative to the direction of travel.

Each definition of attitude is worthy of study, but let's focus on 5 and discuss how it relates to your body language in sales. We don't need to be aeronautical engineers to know that the orientation of the nose of an airplane in relation to the ground has everything to do with the success or failure of flight. An attitude that is too high may have the same ill effect on flight as one that is too low, i.e. both could result in a crash landing.

The same could be said for the impact one's attitude may have on sales performance. For a moment, look in the mirror, assume you are an airplane, and adjust your attitude by raising and lowering your chin. Take note of the position of your chin and let's discuss what it might suggest about your demeanor.

First let us address the shortcomings of a chin that is held too high. Imagine the character Thurston Howell III from the 1960's television series *Gilligan's Island*. The actor who portrayed this character deliberately raised his chin in an exaggerated manner to convey his assumed superiority over his fellow castaways. Raise your chin as high as possible, push your shoulders back, and speak as if you are a millionaire yourself. Do you feel a bit full of yourself? Are you projecting overconfidence or even dominance, perhaps in a way that might be inauthentic or offensive to those around you? Now drop your chin to your chest, cast your eyes downward and say aloud, "I am the greatest!" Do you still feel like a million bucks? I would say that the likelihood is that you don't feel that way at all. You might have spoken the words, but your body language was sending a clear, non-verbal message that had significantly devalued your declaration.

Would you trust, or be more likely to purchase a product from a person who displayed either one of these extreme attitudes? Probably not. But you may adjust your attitude and stride more confidently into any situation without saying a word. A person whose chin is moving upward is perceived as confident and in control. A person whose chin is moving downward is perceived as shy and subordinate. Which position do you think would be most likely to elicit a "yes" from your prospects?

You may be hesitant to adopt mannerisms that at first feel awkward to you, but with practice you will see a significant difference in how you are perceived by others. Here is what is going to happen now:

1. The next time you are in front of a prospect, you will be thinking about the attitude of your chin.

2. You will find yourself raising your chin ever so slightly as you introduce yourself.

3. You will have a grin on your face, clearly amused by how silly you feel.

4. That on-the-verge-of-laughter grin is going to translate into a more confident you.

5. You will feel confident and your prospect will feel at ease.

The only way to know this for sure is to deliberately try it and consciously find your authentic silly chuckle for yourself. As one who has left innumerable sales calls thinking, "I can't believe that worked," I can attest that this simple attitude adjustment does work when put into practice. Many sales reps have told me that they have enjoyed going on calls with me, since they enjoy being part of a team that displays positive energy and enthusiasm. They have told me that they have also found it helpful to see that our upbeat attitudes have positively impacted the prospects, and as a result, had decidedly sped up the sales process. In a phrase, what I'm suggesting is that no matter how "important" the sales call may be, do not be afraid to still have fun.

It's important to note that people are predisposed to respond in kind - this is human nature. Laughter, tears and enthusiasm are in fact incredibly contagious. Similarly, appearing subordinate or disappointed will never earn you the role of leader in a discussion. If you want to win, lead with your chin, be quick to smile, even a laugh, and always enter the room with the highest level of enthusiasm.

Act 4

Me First

Like it or not, we live in a "Me First" world and good sales-people should take great care to leverage this fact to their full advantage.

When Barack Obama ran for President of the United States in 2008, his candidacy was far from assured. Beyond the usual party-line protests, he was challenging the fact that no Black Person had ever held the country's highest office. Additionally, he was running on a resume that featured the least executive leadership experience of any prior President. Nonetheless, he decidedly won the election.

Candidate Obama knew that while he was on the campaign trail, every trip to the podium represented a sales opportunity. His brilliant campaign slogan, "Yes We Can," resonated with the "Me First" attitude of a majority of voters and gave him an advantage over the competition. When he famously said,

"This election is not about me. This election is about you," his poll ratings soared, pushing him far ahead of his primary challenger.

I believe that Barack Obama won the Presidency - not because he was the most qualified candidate - but because he was the best salesperson in the race. He was able to masterfully redirect questions about his qualifications by reiterating again and again what he would do for the American people if elected. And today, even with a declining popularity and growing discontent, President Obama continues to push his message that he is committed to making life better for you and me.

Unlike the President, most salespeople fail to recognize the importance of ensuring that their prospects recognize their "Me First" advantage. If you are only focused on achieving your assigned quota or sales goal, i.e. that your objective is to simply get the sale, you are not considering the needs of your prospect. Your prospect must be fully convinced that you are more interested in his or her needs than in your own success.

Using WIIFM

I can promise you that Barack Obama would never have won the Presidency if his core message had been "I want to be President so that I could play golf whenever, wherever, and with whomever I wish." His message had been carefully constructed to appeal to people's desire for their own well-being. Voters had their eyes on WIIFM, asking "If I vote for him, What's In It For Me?"

To personally experience WIIFM, take a look at a group photograph that includes you. Did you notice where your eyes went first? Undoubtedly, you immediately looked at yourself to see how YOU looked in the photo. It didn't matter that you were holding a beautiful baby, even if that baby was your own son or daughter. Regardless of who else was in the photo, your initial concern was whether your hair looked good or if your smile was broad enough. In other words, you were exhibiting "Me First" behavior.

Frankly, it's simply human nature to want to look at our own picture first. And when selling, it is also important to remember the following quote, which I have taken the liberty to amend:

"No one cares how much you know (or what you think),
until they know how much you care (about them)."
- Theodore Roosevelt

For example, good doctors, like good salespeople, know that it is important to address a patient's concerns if they are to gain the trust that is required to get to the next steps, i.e. to discuss what is ailing the patient and then what could be done to improve his or her condition.

Although the questions may be different in nature, salespeople may and should proceed the same way as a doctor. If for example, you are selling medical devices, in order to establish the credibility you need to educate a physician prospect on your products, you must first show them that you care about them, their practices, their employees, and of course, their patients. Your focus must never be on what you think about the product you're selling, what you have been trained to say about the product, or what a completed sale would mean for you. Your focus must be on discovering what your prospects need. Only at that point will they be able to think about it as a solution.

Rather than making a bold statement like, "This is the greatest medical breakthrough ever," you must lead your prospects to this conclusion by asking questions, providing facts, and getting them to speak about how your product benefits them. The more they speak, the more trust is gained, and the sooner you will discover their true objections.

To help master this strategy, try meeting with your sales manager prior to your next few sales calls and share exactly what you are planning to say and what you would like your prospects to say in return. Think about what might be your prospects' WIIFM and go to the call with the goal of getting them to *tell you* why they need your product, instead of having to *sell them* on why they must have it.

Take ACT-ion

For this act's ACT-ion, you will again need a pencil and paper. For now, forget the objections your prospects might have and write down a list of all the good things that may and should happen if your prospects elect to do business with you. In other words, write down what's in it for *them*. Now, decide exactly how you are going to communicate this to them, appealing directly to their "Me First" mentality. With an effective delivery, they will know that you care about them and will be excited to hear what you have to say.

Act 5

Today is Gregarious Day

Have you ever counted the number of people with whom you speak on an average day? Most of us think we talk to many folks on a daily basis. But the truth is that we pass by the majority of those we encounter without saying a word, and miss the opportunity to convey a simple hello or kind comment that might have improved both their day and ours. If you want to hear the word "yes" more often in your personal and professional life, make today *Gregarious Day* and bring an outgoing, enthusiastic attitude to every public interaction you both encounter and create.

A simple trick I like to use that helps me to be gregarious, even when I'm not really in the mood, is to shift my behavior from that of a guest to that of a host. What is guest behavior? When invited to be a guest in another person's home, we automatically shift into this mode (also known as best behavior), but who could be truly comfortable in situations where our best behavior is required? When your host insists that you "make yourself comfortable" or "make yourself at home," do you really do that?

When I make myself comfortable in my own home, I'm on the couch with my shoes off, flipping through the channels with the TV remote, and I am certainly never worried if my drink is on a coaster. As a visitor, we have been trained (thanks, Mom) to default to guest behavior, which means we become more "well-behaved," but less relaxed. We also become less outspoken and opinionated. Even if we would like something as insignificant as more cream in our coffee, we probably wouldn't ask for it. We would just drink our coffee a little too black for our taste, or only drink a few sips and pretend that we just weren't very thirsty.

The obvious downside of guest behavior is that it relegates us to a subordinate role that often puts us in an uncomfortable position. A good host, who is also striving to be polite, would be horrified if he or she thought; "Jim isn't comfortable in my home? Well why didn't he say something?"

As a result, we are more comfortable and have more fun when we are playing host. As a host, we have the opportunity to be welcoming, outgoing, and eager to serve our family, friends, and acquaintances. In other words, we want everyone to have a good time. We insist that our guests get comfortable, and even double down on our efforts to make it happen. Host behavior enables us to be in charge of the room. So, if you want to generate more business and close more deals, you must demonstrate confident and welcoming host behavior, even when you are a "guest" in your prospect's office.

If you have ever dined with me, you would have seen host behavior in action, but it took time and effort for me to develop that more outgoing and engaging personal brand. That effort has been worth it; since becoming more gregarious, I have enjoyed significant personal, social and financial rewards, simply by being seen as a leader. Below are some simple practices you could begin to use today in your effort to become gregarious, in all your interactions:

1. With rare exception, you should never dine alone. Pick a customer, a prospect, a friend, a co-worker, your spouse, or anyone else with whom to dine. Use meal times to get to know someone better. Always. Dining alone is a poor use of our short time on earth.

2. When dining out, always say hello to your server as soon as you are seated. If possible, address the server by his or her first name, politely and with a smile. **Remember, you are not a guest at the table. You are the host.** If your server isn't wearing a name badge or you don't know his or her name, ask for it. Then as a good host, introduce yourself and everyone else at the table. And don't just use the server's name once – call the server by name at every opportunity. Practice makes perfect and this daily hosting practice will pay huge dividends as

you learn how to make everyone around you feel comfortable, happy and more willing to serve you. This will translate to your selling skills in no time.

3. Next, ask your server to do something that will enable him or her to participate in your enjoyment of the restaurant, e.g. "Joanna, what is your favorite item or best thing on the menu?" A good server will know how to respond. Good hosts however, never judge or otherwise belittle or demean their server, even if they don't react well. Your job is to be kind to your server under any circumstance if only to be kind, and to ensure that you get the very best service.

4. At the end of the meal, always pick up the check. Yes, you. This is the role of the host, and in the grand scheme of business and life, the cost of a meal is negligible compared to the rewards that will follow. Do this at every meal and don't expect someone else to pay the next time you go out for a meal. As a host, it is always your turn to take the lead.

Trust me when I tell you that your kindness as a good host will be returned to you tenfold, even with complete strangers. Your generosity, especially when it's not expected, will be recognized by all and serve you well in the future.

For further proof that this concept holds true, next time you're at a bar, randomly buy a round of drinks for the people seated to your left and to your right and then watch what happens. Being gregarious for no reason is life-affirming fun and well worth the price when considering the good feelings, new conversations, and new business and referrals that your more outgoing attitude will generate.

Opportunities to employ these practices and similar acts of gregariousness are presented to you every day and you should strive to make them part of your personal brand. By doing so, you will never miss a chance to be viewed as the leader of all your interactions. Over time, these habits will become second nature and flow quite naturally into your business life.

Being the Host at Trade Shows

Sales representatives at trade shows are perhaps the best example of how *not* to use the host technique. Although everyone wears a name badge and seems eager to meet and network with new people, I have actually found the behavior of sales representatives here, to be extremely disappointing. If you walk from sales booth to sales booth, take notice of the number of reps who are standing around with their arms crossed, speaking mostly to their fellow reps and only entering into conversations with others when initiated by an interested prospect or passerby. As a salesperson, I cannot fathom why any rep would choose to play the role of guest or act as if he or she were on a company-paid vacation. Working at trade shows is difficult, and when on the floor, salespeople should always play the role of host.

To avoid falling into this trap, be gregarious. Glance at a

random person's name badge and say, "Hi Jennifer. I see you work for XYZ Corp. Tell me, what do you do for them?" Quite naturally, a conversation will ensue. As befits a good host, you would be taking the initiative to reach out to Jennifer to make her feel comfortable, and perhaps in the process, open the door to acquiring a prospect, referral source or at the least, a new acquaintance.

Since opportunities for these "name badge interactions" occur on a daily basis, e.g. at a trade show, a retail store, or even a restaurant, I would encourage you to take advantage of each and every one of them. As a personal reminder, remember this simple phrase:

"If you SEE the name on the name badge, SAY the name!"

Putting this concept into practice is easy and may also be fun. Most people usually forget that they are even wearing a name badge. Calling out, "Hey John" when John passes by will most likely lead him directly to you in his effort to figure out where the two of you might have met (although you have never even met each other).

Second Nature

After only a few attempts at being gregarious and employing host behavior, you will discover that using this technique will quickly help to build your confidence in your ability to speak with total strangers, which is a key element to successful cold calling in sales. With continued practice, you will be leading discussions with a level of confidence and charisma that commands the attention of your prospects and as a result, causes them to follow your lead. By doing this, the next time you have the opportunity to present to a key decision-maker, you will find yourself speaking with greater ease and a closing mentality, knowing that you have done it so many times before. It will be second nature.

Take ACT-ion

This Act's ACT-ion is to select one day this week to be your *Gregarious Day*, a day in which your job is to speak to as many people as possible - especially to people you do not know - and to attempt to lead each and every dialogue or interaction. If today is your chosen day (and why not today?), get started now by introducing yourself to the person sitting or standing next to you, and remember to be your brand. Put a smile on your face, use a friendly yet persuasive tone of voice and employ body language that would make it very difficult for them to say "no" to your invitation to talk. You will be amazed at the difference that just one *Gregarious Day* may make for you as well as for those recipients of your outward kindness to make their day just a bit brighter.

Act 6

Those Voices in Your Head

Now that we have discussed the importance of a positive appearance and demeanor, let's examine those voices in your head that might be hindering your success. Allow me to present a mental exercise that has been positively impacting lives for generations and has worked in every possible situation to counter any negative or sheepish attitudes. Regardless of your religious beliefs, your task is to simply memorize the first four lines of the Serenity Prayer:

God grant me the serenity
To accept the things I cannot change;
Courage to change the things I can;
And wisdom to know the difference.

These are powerful words. So powerful in fact, that they have been widely embraced by Alcoholics Anonymous since the early 1950s. Although this prayer might have religious overtones, its message may also be powerful in helping to sort complex life events into three easy-to-manage categories. The prayer continues:

Living one day at a time;
Enjoying one moment at a time;
Accepting hardships as the pathway to peace...

Most salespeople roll their eyes when I refer to this part of the prayer - not because they don't believe in the message, but because they don't want to hear it. I generally reference these words when speaking about situations in their lives that I know they cannot control. Quoting from the Serenity Prayer seems to be more effective than telling them to "be glad it's not ten million dollars" when they learn that their new quota has become more than double the amount of the prior year's sales. As for the events we cannot change - the loss of a job, divorce, illness, or even a death in the family - the message is that we must accept them and move on to Plan B as soon as possible.

This strategy works well when a salesperson receives a "no", since it would be a waste of time and energy discussing the potential for a different outcome when it could not be changed. For example, if you drop a beer bottle, it will break into pieces. The force of gravity ensures that result and there is nothing you could do about it. Once the bottle is broken, it would seem to make sense that you would try to figure out how to clean up the broken pieces. Yet, our natural inclination would be to try to figure out the cause of the break, instead of focusing on the solution.

In general, wasting time discussing things that cannot be changed may take up a good portion of a salesperson's day. We must resist this time wasting urge to discuss things that we cannot change. When something goes wrong, when someone is down, or when less than desirable events occur, refer to the Serenity Prayer as a basis for action and ask yourself:

1. Could it be changed?
2. If so, how?
3. Does this stink? (Go ahead and vent for a moment)
4. How do we move forward from here?

The more quickly we accept the things we cannot change, the better off we will be, even if the hand we have been dealt is a lousy one. Some measure of venting is inevitable, but just venting won't accomplish anything positive. Take note of this human behavior at your next gathering of fellow sales team members, a meeting at which everyone seems predisposed to complain about something related to the challenges of the job or even about the employer who is paying for the gathering. Here's a phrase I often use to counter this negative use of time and energy:

> *"People only vent to other people who*
> *essentially can do nothing about it."*

Keep this phrase in mind the next time you or someone you know is spending valuable time venting. Every time someone gets on a negative roll while in my presence, I repeat it to myself, and it always makes me smile. I could listen and I may even empathize, but if you're spending time venting to me about a problem, there is usually nothing I could do about it. I would like to share with you the names and authors of several books I have found to be of value that discuss ways to counter the human biochemical reaction that occurs during the venting process.

Oh F#@& to OK

"Amygdala hijack" is a medical term popularized by Daniel Goleman in his 1995 book, *Emotional Intelligence: Why It Can Matter More Than IQ.* In summary, the author explains that during times of increased stress, something called amygdala fluid washes over the area of the brain that controls logical reasoning, temporarily suspending one's ability to control emotions. The greater the stress, the more amygdala fluid is generated and the more likely we are to revert to basic animalistic instincts. Essentially, we are left with two choices - fight or flight.

In his book, *Just Listen*, author Mark Goulston addressed the issue of reacting to "trigger happy" with anger and negativity. Goulston suggested that the best way to control this negative inclination would be to learn a process that would move yourself from "Oh F#@& to OK" in the least amount of time. The process would actually control the flow of amygdala fluid that washes the control of our emotions down the drain.

To illustrate, assume that you discover a flat tire on your car. Needless to say, you would not be happy. Most of us would be triggered to experience an emotion ranging from moderate frustration to all out anger ("Oh F#@&"). But eventually, your brain would shift into a mode that is focused exclusively on the solution. So although you may still be frustrated, you would begin to calm down and focus on what's next. After a period of time, the tire would get repaired and your vehicle would be back on the road. At that point, you might still be unhappy, but now it's "OK." So if we could travel from "Oh F#@& to OK" in the time it takes to change the tire, why couldn't we do it that quickly in our business lives and save us (and everyone else) from unnecessary drama?

When a problem arises in sales (which is generally when a "no" is received), our brains function best when trying to solve the problem. As a result, it makes the most sense to try to reach the solution as soon as possible. This way of thinking is especially valuable for some salespeople whose natural tendency is to react to adversity with negativity. In turn, their negativity would quickly diminish the positive energy that would be required to get where they needed to go. And so, these folks head in the exact opposite direction of others who are more successful. As part of my conventional coaching, I have always advised salespeople to *take the emotion out of the deal*, which is exactly the goal of both the Serenity Prayer and the solution-based approach.

Every Storm Runs Out of Rain

When you find yourself becoming increasingly frustrated, another practice that would help to reduce and/or eliminate excessive emotion would be to adopt a "this too shall pass" attitude. Simply ask yourself if you would feel the same way about your negative situation tomorrow, or next week, or next month or even next year. As impossible as the situation might seem to you at that moment, e.g. like a good hard rain in the middle of your overnight camping trip, most stress inducers will eventually pass. Can't find a job? You will. Can't close the deal? You'll get the next one. Hate your job? Hate your life? Maybe your feelings are real or maybe they're imagined, but whatever the situation; remember that even the worst life crises somehow dissipate over time.

Take ACT-ion

Your ACT-ion for this Act is very simple: Learn the first four lines of the Serenity Prayer and put them into practice. Write down the top three stressors in your business life that may be hindering your progress toward achieving your sales goals. Then, as the prayer dictates, accept the things you cannot change, change the things you can, and pray for the wisdom to know the difference.

Act 7

Putting a "Yes" in the Bank

Most salespeople would agree that there is nothing worse than a long sales cycle. I used to think that way too, until I learned how to put a "yes" in the bank. Over time, after making multiple deposits, you will begin to view your sales career as a process of making "yes" withdrawals when you need them, rather than waiting for the critical times when you are faced with the need to urgently close deals. By banking "yesses," you will build a solid future. But in order to get to this point, you must develop patience with the sales cycle and learn how to turn your "not now" prospects of today into your "right now" sales of tomorrow.

Simmer is Part of the Recipe

When I have been asked how long it typically takes to close

a sale, my answer is always the same: "It depends. Two weeks, two months, or two years." And that answer applies to the sale of any product or service. For example, a real estate agent might say that selling a house takes a long time. However, that same agent may also tell you about a property on which he or she received multiple offers and ended up selling in a single day.

There is no right answer to how long a sale *should* take. Personally, I have always let my prospects know that I would be happy to work within any timeframe. But even in those situations, I have outlined the necessary steps they would need to take if they did decide to engage that day or within two weeks. In real estate, even a quick closing needs a signed contract, an inspection, a title search and other required paperwork - steps that often take two weeks or more. So it's important to let prospects know the process for completing the transaction, even if it does take some time to reach a decision.

All prospects know that salespeople, by their very natures, have objectives. They also know that salespeople would rather secure them as customers today instead of tomorrow. But by letting them know that we understand that "simmer is part of the recipe," we could create a trusting environment that is more conducive to closing a sale, regardless of when it happens.

If your dinner depends on the sale, it may be ready quickly, but it also might get burned in the process. Many a supervisor, board member, investor, or other third party connected to a sales process have pressed me to "hurry up." But no one can thaw a frozen deal faster than me, the salesperson, the one person who intimately understands the inside details of the transaction.

Be Patient

Great things come to those who are willing to wait. My biggest client to date (the client generated $32 million in recurring sales over a seven-year partnership) immediately informed me that because his organization was so large, it would take three years to make a buying decision. Today, he and I both laugh about how the younger me thought at the time, "Yeah, right!" But that's exactly what happened. I put his "yes" in the bank, continued to foster the relationship and eventually enjoyed the reward that came to me after waiting three years – a reward of seven years of recurring commissions. That's one "yes" I am very happy to have put in the bank.

In sales, timing is everything. There will be a sales quota assigned this year, next year and every year thereafter, so putting "yesses" in the bank today is critical if you are to achieve your assigned objectives of tomorrow. Remember that everyone you meet is either a prospect or a referral source and that getting a "no" is okay, for it might just mean "not today." Embracing this notion removes the pressure from selling and ensures that no single deal becomes a must-have.

Remember also that any pressure you might be feeling when conducting a sale is likely going to be visible to your prospect. If at any time, your prospect gets the sense that you *need* the deal, it could cause him or her to speculate on why that might be the case. The bottom line is that prospects are never comfortable with salespeople who display excessive urgency. Sell as if you have all of the time in the world, whether that is or is not the situation. This relaxed attitude will help your prospects to feel in control and eventually help them make the quick decision for which you had hoped in the first place.

Take ACT-ion

So here is this Act's ACT-ion: 1) Open a "Bank of Yes" account today; 2) Make a short list of places at which you know you'll eventually get a "yes", even if it's not now; and 3) Resist the urge to be overly eager to get those "yesses." Instead, put them in the bank for a future withdrawal. Make as many "yes" deposits as possible and always keep your bank register nearby for easy review. Over time, with perseverance and an all-the-time-in-the-world attitude, you will be able to withdraw your "yesses" at times when you need them the most.

Act 8

Establishing EBS (Equal Business Stature)

When it comes to conducting business, an individual's social status, lofty professional title or even fancy car or home are irrelevant. In business, regardless of the product or service that is being sold or shared, everyone has EBS or Equal Business Stature. In our daily lives, we should all strive to achieve EBS. Otherwise, and particularly in businesses in which prospects have a perceived upper-tier status, we might find ourselves relegated to a subordinate position in a discussion. If this is the case, you may usually expect to see a slow-down of the sales cycle and eventually, to receive a "no".

Undoubtedly, you have read multiple books and articles on peer-to-peer selling, i.e. VP-to-VP or CEO-to-CEO sales calls. Frankly, I find the notion that your CEO needs to speak with your prospect's CEO to be ludicrous. As professional salespeople, we have the products and services that our prospects and customers need to be successful. In fact, the only way that they may acquire these products and services is through us. As a result, we actually become one of the most important, if not *the* most important component of the process. As buyers, some people don't like automotive salespeople. But if you need a new vehicle, you won't drive off the lot without the help they do provide.

Once we, as salespeople, understand that we have EBS, the dynamic of the sales interaction changes. The situation is no longer Little You vs. Big Them. Instead it becomes two equally important business people working together to make or save money, to improve process efficiencies or to find a solution together they might never have considered. Once you internalize the notion of EBS, your sales results will soar. There would be no one person with whom you may not see or interact, especially since you know that your visit and presentation would add real value to his or her business.

Take a moment to process and own this concept before going to your next sales appointments, and walk into those meetings with the knowledge that 1) You are on equal footing with the prospect; and 2) What you have to share is at least as important, if not more important, than whatever your prospect might perceive as their other priority.

Good Apples

I frequently reference Apple Store salespeople in my

training sessions because I believe that they do their jobs exceedingly well. Walk into an Apple Store, and you will quickly discover that the store's team members possess expert knowledge about the products they are selling. But I have also found it ironic that based on an assumption of their average wages, many of those salespeople might not even be able to buy the very products they are selling if not for their employee discounts.

My point is that although the salespeople at the Apple Store might not be perceived as having the same business stature as the customers who are buying their products, they command respect based on their expert knowledge. They are extremely enthusiastic about everything Apple and display genuine empathy for those customers who might possess years of life or work experience, but know very little about the products. In other words, these salespeople know that they have the knowledge and information that will make their prospects feel comfortable about saying "yes" to the sale of a premium-priced item.

Similarly, regardless of what you are selling as well as the perceived business stature of your prospect, you are an expert in your field and have valuable information that your decision-makers desperately need. If your product or service would provide a large enough return on investment, you may well be the single most important person with whom he or she speaks all day or maybe even, all year.

Take ACT-ion

For this Act's ACT-ion, write down a list of prospects whom you might have felt were more important than you. When you're done, review the list with your manager and then promptly throw it away. Now go back and view each prospect as someone with whom you have always had EBS or Equal Business Stature. Once you have quietly and confidently declined to be relegated to the subordinate role and begin to sell with the confidence of knowing this to be true, you will vastly increase your chances of closing the deal.

Act 9

Telling Them vs. Selling Them

"People love to buy; they just don't want to be sold."

This quote is so ubiquitous; I was unable to source its original speaker. If you were to think about your own shopping experiences, it would not take too long for you to appreciate the accuracy of this notion. Most of us love to shop and shopping becomes even more fun when there's an emotional or meaningful reason for making a specific purchase. After considering the concept of Equal Business Stature (EBS), it seems to me that the quote would be more valuable if it were appended to say:

> *"People love to buy: they just don't want to*
> *be sold...instead, they want to be told."*

Essentially, I'm suggesting that once mutual trust has been established with a prospect, the selling strategy may change. Rather than trying to sell a prospect on a product, we need to ask the right questions in order to determine what is most suitable for their needs and then simply *tell them* what we recommend.

To illustrate, consider my recent purchase of a new computer. Although I knew that it was time for an upgrade, I knew nothing about the latest hardware offerings. The usual questions emerged: Should I buy a laptop or a desktop? Should I consider a tablet? In either case, do I need a full-sized or a mini? How large of a hard drive do I need? 250GB? 500GB? Wait, what's a Gigabyte again? I realized that I did not have the knowledge required to make a purchase decision and like many shoppers, took my fear of experiencing buyer's remorse right into the computer store. What if I discovered after buying the computer that I actually needed something different, or that I had paid too much, or perhaps that I should have waited for the next version to be released?

In most instances, when it comes to buying, like many buyers, I want to be *told* what to buy and I want to hear it from an expert. I want someone to provide the information I need, not in order to actually make the decision, but to be confident that the decision that will be made for me is the appropriate one. With this in mind, I went to the store and walked out with a new iPad instead of the laptop that I thought I had needed. As a bonus, I even ended up spending less than I had expected when I walked in the door.

As an expert in your field, you possess a wealth of knowledge that enables you to confidently tell your prospects exactly what they should be doing. Rather than pitching them on the features and benefits of your product or service, you should be telling them how it works, why it is effective, and why it would be a tremendous value. This change in strategy, while subtle, will prove highly effective in practice and lead to more closed deals. In retail sales, we are always met with the words, "How can I help you?" Although your selling environment may differ from that of a retail store, you must still have those same words in your own mind when you walk into your meeting.

Take ACT-ion

When you are telling prospects what you would like them to do, do not try to sell them on why they should do it. Instead, say to them, "Let's do this..." followed by your recommendation. By providing your prospects with expert information, you are in essence *telling* them what action to take and simultaneously making them feel like they are making the decision themselves. Employing this Tell Them vs. Sell Them strategy will lead your prospects happily toward the metaphorical cash register to complete the transaction.

For this Act's ACT-ion, let's do the following: Write down how your product or service works and be sure that it may be easily understood. Next, write down everything that makes it extremely effective. Finally, note specifically what makes it an outstanding value. In doing so, you will have provided the foundation for an effective, easily repeatable sales talk that will help get the "yes" that you desire.

Act 10

Happy People Sell More

By now, you have gotten the message that a great attitude is critically important to achieving success in sales. So you might be wondering why we are continuing to spend time talking about it. The answer is simple: Because happy people sell more. We have already discussed the fact that most salespeople waste too much time worrying about things that they cannot control. The following is a derivative thought that warrants discussion and in practice, is designed to put you in charge:

> *"The quality of life is controlled by those few seconds*
> *between stimulus and response. You CAN'T control*
> *the stimulus, but you CAN control your response."*

Memorize this phrase and use it as part of your ongoing effort to remove the emotion from negative situations. It is worth reiterating that reacting to outside stimuli with negativity is never helpful and invariably produces undesirable outcomes. Those who choose to vent their frustrations are often only fueling their own suffering.

Think about it: Does it make sense to swat a gnat with a baseball bat? Of course not, but many people do it anyway. Do referees really end up making better calls when coaches scream at them to the point of getting tossed out of the game? Doubtful. Making a scene might be considered great showmanship or even provide footage for a funny clip on the Internet, but that would be about much as that behavior would accomplish.

It would be easy for us to make excuses for people who allow their emotions to run roughshod over everything around them by arguing that "they're really passionate about the game." But people who behave in this manner probably need to get a better grip on themselves, particularly those adults who would never accept such inappropriate behavior from their own children.

Take ACT-ion

This Act's ACT-ion is to identify instances in your past or current experiences in which you did not deal appropriately with your unhappiness with a situation, and as a result of your behavior, made the situation worse. Did you kick the dog? Yell at your assistant? Explode at the waiter? Even if you were surrounded by bad stimuli in those situations, you would have been better served by invoking a thoughtful, calm response. Taking this positive approach will result in a marked improvement in your quality of life as well as in your success in the selling of your product or service.

Write down three personal experiences of bad stimuli. Next, write down how you responded to each. Finally, write down what would have been a more appropriate response. Adding the words "bad stimulus" into your lexicon will help to remind you that the right response from a happy person, even in a bad situation, may derive a positive outcome from an otherwise negative occurrence. Happy. People. Sell. More.

Part Three

Controlling the Quantity of Your Calls

If you recall from the book's introduction, we discussed that there are only three factors, which we can control as salespeople: Our attitude; the quantity of our calls; and the quality of our calls. Of those three components, developing skills to increase call quantity is the most important. Why? Because even if you have the best possible attitude as well as the best products or services on the market, if you don't have enough prospective buyers, nothing else matters. And without an abundance of calls, the quality of your presentations would never come into play.

Act 11

Setting Quantity Goals

The goal of this Act is to encourage you to begin thinking quantitatively. Thinking this way will allow you to establish a personal goal of the number of prospects that you plan to see on a given day, month and year, with the specific intent of securing a positive outcome. Doing this will give you a clear advantage over the competition, if only that few people take the time to set themselves up with this level of detail.

Do the Math

In order to break records, you have to keep records. In sales, this means that if you do not have specific appointment quantity goals and a way with which to monitor your progress, you are *not* in control of the sales process. You are in essence allowing your professional life to happen to you instead of making it happen for you. Here's a simple method to help you establish your appointment quantity goals and ensure that you are the driver on the road to achievement, rather than a passenger who is unaware of the destination. Let's start by doing the math...

- There are 365 days in a calendar year

- Of those 365 days, 255 are considered business days

- Of those 255, most salespeople reserve 60 days for dedicated office work and internal meetings

- Of the remaining 195 days, most salespeople deduct 30 days for holidays and time with family

- This leaves 165 days per year to see prospects

If you are like most salespeople, you probably think you have plenty of time to get more business into your pipeline. But as you could see from our bullet points, your time is already limited. Since *you alone* are in control of the number of prospects you will attempt to see on those 165 days, you need to answer the following question: "How many NEW prospects could you realistically meet in a single day?"

You might be thinking: "There are too many variables affecting an average day in the field. How could I possibly determine this number? Some days are better than others." Understood, but for the sake of setting your appointment quantity goal (the number of people you will see in person on a run rate basis for the year), let's assume that your answer is "one." Meeting one new prospect per day would equate to setting an annual quantity goal of 165. Obviously, meeting two per day would double it to 330. But imagine if you could meet four new prospects per day - your annual quantity goal would skyrocket to 660. Realistically, due to the size of your territory, it might not even be possible to meet 660 new prospects, but at least you're thinking about the possibilities.

We could do the math together all day, but *you alone* must decide on a realistic quantity goal and *you alone* must establish a plan to achieve it – a plan that would work for all parties (you, the company, and your family). Once your annual quantity goal is set, keep it with you at all times so that it is always accessible when you want to measure your progress. If your personal goal is to see 500 prospects this year, and on July 1, with just two quarters to go, you realize that you have only seen 220, you certainly don't need a manager to remind you that you are running behind schedule.

Monitoring and measuring your progress is no one's job but yours, and the better you do it, the less likely it will be that your manager will be looking over your shoulder. The most successful salespeople always know when it's time for them to work harder and never need to be told to pick up the pace. If you unexpectedly miss a day, waste a day, or lose a day to illness, *you alone* will know what it's going to take to make up for lost time and to get back on track.

Take ACT-ion

This Act's ACT-ion is to do the math and do it now. What is your annual quantity goal? I can assure you that if your answer is not a specific number (meaning that it sounds something like "as many as I can"), then your results will not be very impressive. As a sales coach, I often prepare reps before they go on business travel by asking them how many appointments they have scheduled for the week. If the answer does not include a specific number, I know that the rep is not operating from an organized plan that will help to ensure a successful trip. That rep is only hoping to succeed and as the saying goes, "hope is not a strategy."

Once you have determined your annual quantity goal, write it down and post it where you will see it regularly, i.e. near your desk, or perhaps as the wallpaper on your phone. This will ensure that you remain focused on achieving or exceeding this most important number, one that directly correlates to your level of success.

Act 12

Creating an Active Prospect List

The number one reason some salespeople are less successful than others is that they lack an Active Prospect List.

This simple statement has elicited more protests from sales professionals than any other statement I have made in my sales training sessions. An Active Prospect List is usually perceived as a negative stimulus, a document that salespeople absolutely dread reviewing with their superiors. As a sales coach, I don't see it that way at all. To me, an Active Prospect List represents opportunities to either close a deal or put a "yes" in the bank, and my perspective is that any good salesperson should be excited to share it with his or her manager.

At the same time, good managers should be enthusiastic about sharing strategies and techniques that will help their team members' Active Prospect Lists continue to grow. The discomfort associated with reviewing a prospect list with your manager likely stems from the realization that you simply don't have enough good prospects in your pipeline.

When I randomly ask a salesperson to spend a few minutes with me to go over his or her list, I usually get back a variety of excuses about why he or she doesn't have it on hand. Allegedly, the list is either at home, in the car, on the computer, is a work in progress, or in some cases, doesn't even exist because he or she "knows the territory." It doesn't matter what the reason was for not being able to produce the list. The point is that not having one available for immediate disclosure equates to not having one at all. I have never asked to review a prospect list in order to catch a salesperson without one. I have only asked for it in an effort to help the salesperson work through any current sales and/or accounts which might be stuck somewhere in the Sales Decision Chain.

As we have discussed, setting quantity goals is fairly easy to do, but achieving them requires 100 percent commitment and old-fashioned hard work. An Active Prospect List, loaded with potential prospects, will make the task far easier to accomplish. The challenge is, most salespeople are so busy running around from place to place that they neglect to set aside some quiet time to figure out which of their prospects would be most likely to buy whatever it is that they are selling. So what exactly constitutes an Active Prospect List?

An Active Prospect List...

- Contains no less than twenty-five prospects that you have attempted to contact six times or less over the last ninety days – through any means of communication. In other words, these prospects are considered to be new pursuits.

- A list of *future potential customers.* These prospects do not include people with whom you have already met or have done business or who have said they were ready to do business with you. (All of these people are important too, but for this discussion, we are referring only to the top of the sales funnel.)

- Is organized by those who represent your "soonest revenue" opportunities.

- Contains not just company names, but contact names of individuals at those companies, along with titles, phone numbers, email addresses and whenever possible, the name of the assistant or gatekeeper.

- Has been updated within the last thirty days and contains new prospect names that have been added within the last week. Hence the word "active."

- Is within arm's reach at all times.

- Is extremely familiar to you, because you recognize it as your most important sales document.

- Leads you to speak with brand new prospects for the first time, each and every week.

- Allows you to find order in the chaos and work more efficiently and effectively, to the point where you would not know how to work without one.

There is a very good reason to stop what you are doing and spend a day or even a week creating, organizing and maintaining an Active Prospect List. Without one, you will only find success by what has been given to you instead of what has been earned by you. Taking what you have been given equates to receiving an incoming lead, pursuing it, and closing it. Earning what you want entails influencing many more people than just those who have called in to your office for more information.

If you could choose what you could get, wouldn't you choose to get more than what you're currently getting? If you were truly in charge and not simply reacting to the world around you, would you be more or less efficient with your time? Would you make more or less money? Wouldn't you rather make the easy sales and leave the most difficult customers for later?

Of course you would, and you can do this, as long as you are willing to work hard to accomplish those goals. When you make an effort to talk to more people, you build momentum, and with increased momentum, your territory begins to do the selling for you. By meeting more people, your phone will ring more often and you will have more opportunities to make more sales. By creating an Active Prospect List, you will be well on your way toward achieving your goals.

Take ACT-ion

This Act's ACT-ion is to consider your quantity goal for

next week and ask yourself one question: "Which new prospects do I need to contact in order to reach that goal?" If during the process of creating your short list, you project that next week will be a "bad week" for some reason (reason is a fancy word for excuse), then you may already understand why working from an Active Prospect List is so important.

Remember that your present and future may depend upon the number of sales calls you make each week and that each call you make helps to bolster your job security and that of your co-workers. Just as your hope might be that the shipping department will get your orders out on time, the hope for those people who work in the shipping department is that you will be able to get in front of as many prospects as possible each and every week so that they will have orders to ship. To ensure that you are doing your best, always maintain an Active Prospect List.

Act 13

Defining a Good Prospect

When building your Active Prospect List, you might be thinking: "What exactly constitutes a good prospect?" To help answer that question, let's turn to the experts. In their book, *The New Strategic Selling*, legendary sales trainers Robert B. Miller and Stephen E. Heiman defined four response modes:

- Growth Mode
- Trouble Mode
- Even Keel Mode
- Overconfident Mode

Miller and Heiman believe that prospects buy most often when their businesses are in Growth Mode or Trouble Mode. Therefore, a salesperson who is working from an Active Prospect List must do more than simply control the number of calls being made. He or she must be vigilant in the search for buyers whose businesses are either experiencing growth or are in some sort of trouble that may cause a decline in revenues. In essence, selling becomes a *search process*, one in which we seek out prospects who are most likely to make a near-term purchase, and then we add them to our Active Prospect List.

Too often, we get lost spending time pursuing prospects that we think could benefit from our product (and in fact, might be buyers), but are unwilling to grant us a personal appointment. Often times, it is difficult to get the attention of prospects who are either Even Keel (content with the current situation) or Overconfident (believes that his or her results are better than they are). In either case, these prospects are typically unable to make a near-term decision because they are in a non-buying mode.

As a salesperson, you must have a solid understanding of the defining characteristics of each response mode in order to know a good prospect when you meet one. Because they are the best prospects, let's focus on the ones who fall into the Growth and Trouble Modes, since these targets would be the ones most likely to become your buyers.

Growth Mode

A prospect in Growth Mode wishes to improve their current situation – e.g. get better, faster, stronger, or more profitable - and are ready to invest in the solution. For example, an on-the-rise company might be in need of purchasing such goods and services as office furniture or IT solutions. If a salesperson had what the company needed, he or she could consider it a good prospect. A newly promoted employee would also be someone who is in Growth Mode, because they may be facing unfamiliar products and processes, or perhaps even inheriting the problems of their predecessor. If interest rates dropped suddenly, a mortgage lender might be yet another example of a company in Growth Mode, since this situation might necessitate additional employees or more efficient processes to meet the anticipated increase in demand.

All of the aforementioned are examples of good prospects, and therefore must be on the salesperson's Active Prospect List. Once you have effectively defined who needs your product and who could and would say "yes," you will be able to sell with greater confidence and as a result, generate better results.

Trouble Mode

Although Trouble Mode is often regarded as the opposite of Growth Mode, this is not always the case. Prospects in Trouble Mode are generally feeling the negative effects of external stimuli that are outside their ability to control. We previously learned that having a great attitude and the ability to control our response to bad stimuli might positively impact our success. Similarly, when we encounter prospects who are experiencing a troubling situation, we must be aware of their problems in order to be able to help them find the solution.

For example, if you were to ask most medical professionals for their opinion of the Affordable Care Act, nearly all would say that they are anticipating continuously decreasing reimbursement for the services they have been currently providing. For them, the Affordable Care Act represents an external, negative stimulus that is both beyond their control as well as the cause of additional troubles for their practices. If you were selling a medical device that could generate a new, much-needed, recurring revenue stream for a practice, you could assume that these (troubled) doctors would be good prospects.

Most salespeople instinctively smell opportunity when a new business opens in their territory, but by going one step further and determining the buyer response mode of that business or practice, you may be able to rely on more than luck to either get your "yes" or at the least, get one to deposit in the bank.

Take ACT-ion

This Act's ACT-ion is to review your Active Prospect List and determine which of your current targets are in either Growth or Trouble Mode, and thus represent your most likely near-term business opportunities. Next, write down what you believe to be the reasons that these prospect have landed in either mode and consider how your products or services might help remedy their current situation. By further narrowing the focus of your Active Prospect List, you will guarantee the best use of your time and maximize your sales results.

Act 14

Cold Calling That Works:
Why You? Why Me? Why Now?

No salesperson in the world would be able to achieve an appointment quantity goal without making successful cold calls. But how does a salesperson decide which of the multiple cold call techniques found in various sales literature are the most effective? Personally, I have always encouraged salespeople to focus on mastering just a single technique, which may be used to secure appointments by phone, mail, email, and face-to-face interactions.

Regardless of the medium, all sales communications should be structured in a way that pre-emptively answers three important questions: 1. Why you? 2. Why me? 3. Why now? Additionally, you should make every effort to include the words "good news" and "new information" in your sales communications in order to pique the curiosity of your prospects. Think about a novel that you would describe as a page-turner. It most likely provides just enough information to intrigue its readers and leave them wondering about what might happen next. Great authors lead readers to turn pages all night long. In sales, the most effective way to reveal what's on the next page would be through a personal appointment, which would also help you to meet your appointment quantity goals.

Sharing Good News and New Information on the Phone

Before they make a cold call on the telephone, well-prepared salespeople have a plan, which includes what they would like to accomplish on the call and what they are going to say when they reach the decision maker. This plan also includes a rehearsed script, which would be used if they ended up being redirected to voicemail. Employing the words "good news" or "new information" in a "Why you? Why me? Why now?" format will send the prospect a convincing message that by speaking with you they would have more to gain than to lose. If you properly deliver your message, the prospect will be eager to return your call, since he or she had been left wondering what might be on the next page. Below is a typical telephone script:

You: Hello Mrs. Jones. The reason for my call
is that I have some good news for Mr. Owner
regarding [the subject matter of your product].

Office Manager: Sure, what is the news?

You: Well, the news is really for Mr. Owner, with whom we recently chose to speak due to his reputation in the local community (why you). I expect that he's going to be very excited about what I have to share. May I please speak with him?

Office Manager: I'm sorry, but he's busy. May I ask what this is about?

You: Of course. I have some new information to share that will help expand his customer base through a new product that we are offering exclusively (why me) to select business owners like him. Is there a time when he either takes or returns phone calls?

Office Manager: He usually does that on Wednesday afternoons. May I tell him more about this?

You: Yes. My name is Jim, and I was asked to share this new information with him immediately because we are expanding (why now) into his market this month. Because of his reach in the community (why you), I was told that I should speak with him (why me) the next time I'm in town (why now). My number is 555-123-4567. The businesses with whom I have already spoken have been quite interested, and I'm confident that he will feel the same way, too.

Office Manager: Thank you Jim. I will give him the message.

You: Thank you Mrs. Jones. I also look forward to meeting you when I'm in town. When I see Mr. Owner, I'll be sure to let him know that you were very helpful.

Although this script may be a bit too detailed, I have presented it this way in order to illustrate that when you are trying to reach new people, you are not selling the benefit of your product or service. You are only selling good news and new information in an effort to generate enough curiosity from your prospect to result in an appointment. Any time that you provide the specifics of what you're selling, you forfeit the opportunity to create a page-turning event and make it more difficult to secure an appointment.

Should you reach voicemail, leaving message after message is not an effective way to soften any prospect. Never leave more than one message every couple of weeks; any more will be an enormous turn-off and might even result in causing you to be labeled a "sales stalker." When you do leave a message, make sure it is an effective one since it might be your only shot at piquing the interest of the prospect. And remember, less is more. Leaving just a bit of information will whet the recipient's appetite and cause him to either make the return call or to be available the next time you try to reach him.

"Hello Mr. Owner, it's Jim, your [company] rep. Sorry I missed you, but please call me back when you have a moment since I have some good news and new information to share. Because of your reach in the local community, I think you'll be very excited to hear about this opportunity. When you get a minute, please call me at 555-123-4567."

Sharing Good News and New Information via Email

The rise of email has caused a reduction in the use of the telephone and has not served the sales process well. Many salespeople use email as a crutch and some use it almost exclusively to communicate with prospects. Prospects also cite the use of email as the reason they rarely accept phone calls. Since the resulting lack of personal interaction makes selling extremely difficult, I would like to address the appropriate use of email in securing new appointments.

Since your focus must always be on appointment quantity, you should *never* write a sales email from scratch. Doing so increases the likelihood of typographical and contextual errors, and just as importantly, wastes valuable time that could negatively impact your quantity efforts. A pre-written email template provides you with a safe, repeatable process that would serve you well each day.

One of the best appointment setters I have known is a former colleague who maintains a highly disciplined practice of sending five emails in the morning, five emails before he eats lunch and five emails just before the end of his day. Since he uses a template, it only takes him a few minutes to execute the task. Not surprisingly, his sales pipeline is always full. I haven't seen him in several years, but I have purchased from him twice - each time after receiving the same reminder email.

Here are a few rules for creating an effective email template:

1. Treat your subject line with care. Say too much and the email will not get opened.

2. Everyone is busy, so get right to the point. Start with something like "The reason for this email is..." or "I'm writing to..."

3. Share good news and new information.

4. Skip the niceties. There will be plenty of time later in the process for pleasant exchanges about life.

5. End with an action item.

6. Be sure to use a standard signature with your contact information.

7. Reiterate the message in a P.S.

Incorporating these tips, an effective email template might look like this:

Subject: Good News for Customers Who are Reluctant to Use Your Product

Mr. Owner, I'm writing to share some exciting information about a new, recurring revenue product that is expanding the market for businesses like yours by 20 percent and more, while at the same time improving customer retention.

Could you please point me to the person who could best use this information? Forwarding this email or letting me know a good time for us to speak would be appreciated.

At your service,

Jim Wrigley
jim@mycompany.com
(555) 123-4567

P.S. My last client actually improved his market share by 25 percent...I'm confident that we could do the same for you!

Sharing Good News and New Information on a Cold Call

Similar to our discussion of using telephone and email communications, successful in-person cold calling is also about having a plan. But the plan here is simple: Don't pass by a prospect without stopping in to say hello. This rule is of particular importance for salespeople who often fly and then drive to visit prospects. Making a point to stop in and see your prospects will do wonders toward achieving your appointment quantity goal.

The best way to avoid driving past a prospect is to have both your Active Prospect List and a physical prospect/client map of your territory in hand. Working without either document would be highly inefficient. On your map, draw a clover-leaf or traveling route that will allow you to see both existing clients (as they are great referral sources) and new cold call prospects on every pass. Keep showing up and eventually they will see you. Keep seeing them and eventually they will buy.

Here's a typical cold call script that might be employed when speaking with a gatekeeper:

Hi. My name is Jim and I'm with [company]. I'm here to discuss a new, recurring revenue product that is expanding the market for businesses like yours by 20 percent and more, while at the same time improving customer retention (why you).

Unfortunately, my time is very limited today, but since I'm the one representing this opportunity, I wanted to at least drop by (why me).

Here is my card. I would appreciate it if you would kindly pass it on to Mr. Owner. What is the normal procedure for setting up a discussion with him? I could schedule a phone call or a time to come back later today (why now). Which would he prefer?

By using an effective script at each stop, you will begin to fill your appointment calendar and move more swiftly toward achieving your quantity goal. Of course, as with any technique, there will still be times when you will fail to get a prospect's attention. In those cases, repeated efforts will be required. It is all too common for a salesperson to simply report that "[prospect] did not call back," as if his or her task had been finished after too few attempts. Studies have shown that salespeople who attempt to reach someone *six times* will get an audience 90 percent of the time. Six may seem like a high number, but if that's what it takes to get your audience, my guess is that you won't regret having made a single call.

Take ACT-ion

So here is this Act's ACT-ion: Since no one knows your space and your prospects better than you do, construct both a voicemail script and an email template that will pique the curiosity of your prospects and cause them to "turn the page" or schedule an appointment. Be sure to use the "Why You? Why Me? Why Now?" format and keep your message as simple as possible. Try out your email with several prospects and continue to refine it until you begin to elicit the responses you desire. As for the phone script, remember that practice makes perfect, so rehearse it thoroughly before putting it to use. I'm confident that you will discover few people who will resist the desire to receive a bit of *good news*, or dismiss you if you have some *new information* to share that might be of benefit to them.

Act 15

The Telephone Tracker

Now it's time to employ a bit of old-school "technology" to help improve your sales results. Not long ago, a co-worker of mine made the mistake of leaving what I'm about to introduce on the coffee table in his home office. His wife found it when he was just three weeks into his plan – a plan that designated each Friday as a day to focus on making new sales calls and building his Active Prospect List. On those Fridays, he would lock himself in his office, break only for lunch, and work hard to overcome his reluctance to make cold calls.

One Friday night at dinner, after a long day on the phone, his wife (his true sales manager) asked him how many calls he had made that day; how many decision makers he had reached; and how many meetings he had scheduled for the following week. Although it was nice that my co-worker's wife had cared enough about him to inquire about his progress, my co-worker's Telephone Tracker was not intended to be anyone else's measuring device, but his.

Some micromanagers would love to use the Telephone Tracker to monitor you, measure your activity and perhaps support their belief that you are unable to effectively manage your own sales activity. But make no mistake about it. This rudimentary productivity tool is not for managers (or spouses for that matter). As previously discussed, it is not their job to monitor your activity – YOU ALONE must do that.

The Telephone Tracker will help you focus on what you *should* be doing, especially on days when you would rather be doing something else. So on a Friday, when it's beautiful outside and there is someone or something luring you away from your desk, use this simple tool to help keep you on track. With disciplined execution, it will be a key contributor to your increased income, year after year.

Take ACT-ion

Remember that in order to break records, you have to keep records, so here is this Act's ACT-ion: Mark the next four Fridays in your calendar as days that you will utilize the Telephone Tracker found on the next page. Many scoff when they first see it, noting the fact that it is overly simplistic and outdated when compared to other available productivity tools. But you shouldn't be so quick to dismiss it, for it has been proven, time and again, to help salespeople make more money. Using the Telephone Tracker may be fairly intuitive, but for the sake of instruction, here are some pointers. First, make your own version and print out a copy to use for each of the next four weeks. Next, when you make calls, reach prospects, talk with decision makers and secure sales appointments, simply put a slash through each number you achieve. Review your Tracker at the end of each day, and then again collectively at the end of the four weeks and prepare to experience a world of difference in your quantitative results. Over time, this "old school" device will cause your income to soar.

Telephone Tracker

Day:

Sun   Mon   Tue   Wed   Thu   Fri   Sat

Dials Made:

1 2 3 4 5 6 7 8 9 10 11 12 13 14 15 16 17 18 19 20 21 22 23 24 25
26 27 28 29 30 31 32 33 34 35 36 37 38 39 40 41 42 43 44 45 46 47 48 49 50
51 52 53 54 55 56 57 58 59 60 61 62 63 64 65 66 67 68 69 70 71 72 73 74 75
76 77 78 79 80 81 82 83 84 85 86 87 88 89 90 91 92 93 94 95 96 97 98 99 100

Contacts Reached:

1 2 3 4 5 6 7 8 9 10 11 12 13 14 15 16 17 18 19 20 21 22 23 24 25
26 27 28 29 30 31 32 33 34 35 36 37 38 39 40 41 42 43 44 45 46 47 48 49 50

Decision Makers Spoken To:

1 2 3 4 5 6 7 8 9 10 11 12 13 14 15 16 17 18 19 20 21 22 23 24 25
26 27 28 29 30 31 32 33 34 35 36 37 38 39 40 41 42 43 44 45 46 47 48 49 50

Appointments Secured:

1 2 3 4 5 6 7 8 9 10 11 12 13 14 15 16 17 18 19 20

To-Do List Items Completed Today:

Act 16

Servicing After the Sale

Since getting customer testimonials is part of the repeatable process we must employ to move our prospects toward a final transaction, it is important to consider the level of service provided after the sale that generates these referrals. Let's take another look at each step of the Sales Decision Chain:

1. From **resisting** to **listening**

2. From **listening** to **considering**

3. From **considering** to **willing to do**

4. From **willing to do** to **doing**

5. From **doing** to **glad they did**

6. From **glad they did** to **continuing to do**

7. And finally, to **telling everyone else what they are doing!**

Gathering a notebook of testimonials will help you to achieve your goal of moving a new prospect from Step 1 to Step 4, at which point he or she would make a purchase and become your customer. But the real business - the easy-to-achieve extra dollars you want to extract from your sales territory - emerges when you lead a customer through Step 5, from **doing** to **glad they did**. Getting to this point in the process, i.e. the ultimate objective of any sales rep, is critical since this is the point at which the commissions, bonuses, recognition and other rewards from being percentage-wise better begin. When I say, "I teach salespeople how to earn more money," I know that the areas they can most likely improve upon reside in steps 4 through 7 of the Sales Decision Chain.

Going from **doing** to **glad they did** usually involves the proper implementation, installation, or some other combination of tasks that includes product or service training. In other words, it is critically important that you stick around after you have made the sale. As a sales manager, I've often said to my teams:

"If we don't have utilization, we've got nothing."

In fact, if your customer is not utilizing whatever it is that you have sold him or her, you have worse than nothing - you now have a detractor. To avoid having detractors, Step 5 must be taken very seriously, even if the commission or bonus from a closed deal is already in your pocket.

My strongest advice is to always be sure that your purchaser gets a recognized value from the product or service for what he or she has paid. In order for that to happen, you must pay attention to every detail of the transaction, including the shipping, the installation and the training for how to get the most out of the purchased product or service. As the salesperson, each one of these components is *your* responsibility and *yours alone.*

Personally, I love being the go-to-guy for my customers, and encourage you to feel the same way. If shipping messed up the order, it was *my* fault. If the customer misunderstood something that I thought I had clearly explained, it was also *my* fault. If anyone related to the sale was unhappy about anything, I was absolutely the cause of that unhappiness. By demonstrating this level of personal responsibility to my customers, I prove to them that I will be the *one* person to whom they could turn to get things fixed. Isn't that what you would want, expect and in fact deserve, when you encounter a problem after spending your hard-earned dollars on a new product or service?

Imagine that your brand new car won't start. You just want to get your car up and running again. First you try calling the salesperson who sold you the car, only to be passed along to the service department, and then to the towing company, and finally to a person in the warranty division. Would you be satisfied with this process? Of course you wouldn't. You need a quick solution and want to make only one phone call to the organization that just sold you a $40,000 car. And you want that call to be to the sales associate who sold you the car.

Sadly, it's rare to find sales representatives who are willing to dive head first into handling post-sale problems. They don't seem to understand that when they stand up for their customers, their customers will reciprocate and stand up for them by offering testimonials and referrals that will benefit them throughout their career.

Being present for the customer, post installation, is critical to achieving the final steps of the sales process. The extra time spent with your customers to help them become comfortable with their purchase will go a long way toward increasing your revenue tenfold.

Take ACT-ion

Here is this Act's ACT-ion: Open up your CRM and plan to make more than a few calls today. Contact a mix of your newest customers and several of the older ones with whom you might not have spoken in some time. If you're a sales manager, consider calling some customers who you had not personally sold, if only to introduce yourself and check in with them. Along the way, you'll surely engage in some pleasant conversations as well as experience some negative ones. But don't be discouraged by the negative feedback. Remember that "no" is okay, and usually represents an opportunity to further service a client after the sale and solve a brewing problem that you might not have known even existed.

Act 17

The Importance of Testimonials

We have established that the best salespeople always service their customers after the sale, which occurs in Step 5 and Step 6 in the Sales Decision Chain.

5. From **doing** to **glad they did**
6. From **glad they did** to **continuing to do**

But ask yourself the following, as it relates to the all-important final Step 7, where your customers **are telling everyone else what they are doing**: "When did I receive my last testimonial?" If your answer was "more than two months ago," now is the time to work on getting credit for a job well done by asking your customers for an endorsement of you and your company. Testimonials from other like-minded individuals, similar in size, stature, and daily activities of your new prospects can have a tremendous impact on your success. It goes without saying that you can never have enough customers publicly cheering about you, your products or services, and your company. When a person reads or sees that many others have enjoyed a positive customer experience, they too, quite naturally, become more interested to also get involved.

If you don't think testimonials work, then ask yourself why you see celebrities in print, broadcast and on the Internet endorsing products and services. What is most effective about having a high physical volume of testimonials is that prospects can quickly grasp the notion that you've had plenty of past success, when they see that "everyone" seems to be happy with your work.

Standing Out in a Crowded Field

Displaying a complimentary quote or other form of testimonial from a third party is a terrific way to show the sometimes-small separation between you and the competition, necessary to win the deal. As an example, the following is an actual profile from an online dating site, an extremely crowded and competitive space in which it is exceedingly difficult to stand out. Rather than employing the usual approach of advocating oneself, a forty-something attorney posted testimonials from others to describe her personality. She writes: "Instead of telling you about me, I thought you might like to see what my family and friends say about me. So here's what the survey said you should know:

"She's every guy's Girl That Got Away. Someone please catch her."
– My neighbor, Bruce

"She is the kind of girl every man dreams about. If you don't like beer, wings and football, she's not for you."
– My Colleague, Bill

"Have you heard the song, 'She's everything to me?' I'm pretty sure the artist was singing about her."
– My Friend's Husband, Brian

"Really, dear? Please don't ask me to do this. You're absolutely amazing and you know it."
– My Dad

That is literally "all she wrote." Could you see how her third party testimonials helped to make this attorney seem more interesting than if she had just described herself? If you want to stand out in the crowded field of sales, testimonials can do wonders to get other people's attention.

Take ACT-ion

Here is this Act's ACT-ion: Go get your next testimonial. That task may sound easy, but you will find that it is actually fairly difficult to get even one good written endorsement from your best customer. Why? Because your best customers - the ones with the biggest titles and most influence - are also the people who seem to be the most busy and can't find the time to sit down and write one. And even when they do, I've seen multiple well-intended letters that don't fill the bill, i.e. the letters do not include what we feel is most important to convince other prospects to buy.

In order to avoid this situation, and to make it easy for your customer, write the letter yourself and include exactly what you would like him or her to say. Then, present it for his or her approval using the following script:

"Hi Mr. Owner. I have a small favor to ask. I know you've had some success with our products, and as you probably know, many new prospects often ask if they may speak with our current customers. Rather than asking you to take phone calls, I took the liberty of writing a letter that says what I think you would say about your experience. With your permission, I would like to put it on your letterhead and have you sign it. Of course, please read it over first and make suggested edits. Would that work for you?"

During my twenty plus years of writing realistic testimonials for customers who have enjoyed my products and services, I have never had a request declined or a single word changed. As discussed, the extra revenue and bonus and commission checks, which you are seeking, are hiding in plain sight in Steps 5, 6, and 7 of the Sales Decision Chain. But you must request testimonials from those customers who are now **telling everyone else what they are doing**. Now is the time to make some calls, find your biggest supporters, and do whatever it takes to get their thoughts in writing.

Part Four

Controlling the Quality
of Your Calls

The majority of the training time offered by most organizations is used primarily to educate salespeople on the features and benefits of the products and services they are selling. This section will focus on the quality of our calls and explore techniques for improving the effectiveness of what is said and done during our sales conversations.

Act 18

How to Talk About
What You Do

Nearly every day, someone is sure to ask you what you do, which creates an opportunity to expand your market reach or further your particular cause. Unfortunately, most people fail to derive much value from those one-off discussions.

Whether you are getting on a plane, walking in the park or bellying up to the bar, you should view everyone you meet as either a prospect or a referral source for your business. I'm not suggesting that you should annoy every stranger by chatting about what you do for a living. But I am telling you that there are ways to develop new leads by comfortably and naturally taking advantage of everyday encounters. And because words carry meaning, we must have the right ones ready when given the opportunity to speak.

Ask a Clarifying Question

When asked what you do, replying with, "I'm a sales rep for XYZ Corp" is a sure-fire way to kill a conversation even before it gets started. The right answer must include a deliberately general clarifying question that causes the other party to ask, "How do you do that?"

Asking a clarifying question will help determine whether the person with whom you are speaking is truly interested in your answer. It will also cause him or her to listen attentively, even if he or she initially had no intention to do so. Finally, it will put the focus on the important subject of the discussion - you. Here's an example of how this tactic works in my business of sales coaching:

Them: So what do you do?

Me: You know how just about everybody in business wants to make more money? (The clarifying question)

Them: Sure, I want to make more money too.

Me: Well, I teach people how to do just that.

Them: Really? And how do you do that?

Me: Thanks for asking. I would love to tell you, and depending on what you do, I could probably teach you too."

You might imagine the conversations that might follow, even with a total stranger. By simply asking that person if he or she understands my subject matter, I am able to begin the process of discovering whether he or she could become a prospect or a referral source for my business - either of which would work for me. Of course, not everyone I meet is interested in what I do for a living, but I *have found* that nearly everyone is interested in making more money. And that is the reason why my simple clarifying question almost always works. When I say that I teach people how to increase their income, people naturally wonder how I could do that. It is at that point that they are drawn into **listening** to a story when they otherwise might have **resisted** or not cared at all. Step 1 of the Sales Decision Chain has been achieved by engaging in that random interaction.

In the game of ice hockey, a goal is as good as an assist, since statistically speaking, each is worth one point. Similarly in the world of sales, finding a direct prospect (a goal) should be considered by salespeople to be just as valuable as receiving a referral (an assist), since a point is earned each time you are able to speak about your company or your cause. So the next time you're attending a business event, shopping at the mall or just sitting in a coffee shop, use a clarifying question when asked what you do, instead of relying on the chance that a goal or an assist might happen by itself.

Casting a Big Shadow

Once your prospect or referral source has asked how you do what you do, he or she has no choice but to listen. Therefore, be prepared *in advance* to make your business sound as intriguing as possible. I recommend employing a tactic called "Casting a Big Shadow by Standing Next to the Light" - true stories related to your success that have become the light that makes your shadow (you or your company) seem larger than life. Here's an example of this tactic:

Them: So you teach people how to make more money? How do you do that?

Me: Well, you have probably seen lists of America's fastest-growing companies. I have actually had the good fortune to lead the sales force for one of them, and helped the company develop a unique, scalable selling methodology that vastly improved their sales results.

In that situation, the light that cast my larger than life shadow was that my company had indeed been one of the nation's fastest growing, privately held companies. Fortunately, I actually do have a repeatable and measurable strategy for building any business and I was happy to have been able to implement it at a company whose stock would later become publicly traded. As a result of that experience, I have had this story to share and it has helped to generate scores of business leads, particularly from sales organizations that have been interested in achieving their own exit or liquidity event.

Take ACT-ion

This Act's ACT-ion is to complete a simple, but highly effective exercise. First, write out the clarifying question you will use when someone asks what you do. It will probably begin with something like, "You know how..." followed by a description of a common business problem (i.e. wanting to make more money) that your solution could solve. Then, prepare your follow-up statement to further describe what you do in a manner that casts a big shadow by standing next to the light. Read your response aloud so that you can hear what it will sound like to a third party and repeat the process over and again until your delivery sounds completely natural. With practice, this proven technique will help you gain business opportunities that you never knew existed.

Act 19

Conversation vs. Presentation

One of my favorite pieces of advice about how to make a quality sales call has been to recommend approaching each call as a conversation, rather than as a presentation or demonstration. A high-quality conversation typically involves limited distractions, a series of questions and answers, and the sharing of opinions between two or more parties with varying points of view - all without the expectation of a particular outcome. That's not to say that you don't desire a particular outcome. Of course you want to make the sale, but it's not going to happen unless you create an atmosphere in which there could be a free flow of ideas. By engaging in a typical, casual conversation with a prospect, that prospect will become more comfortable and open to listening to the viability of your solution.

For many people, getting a conversation started is not easy. Even Saturday Night Live, one of America's longest-running television programs, had to figure out the least awkward way to begin the weekly show - its solution was to create a repeatable and highly recognizable process called a "cold open." The producers decided that instead of losing time with a formal introduction, they would have the actors jump right into the first sketch, followed by the phrase, "Live from New York, it's Saturday Night!"

Similarly, salespeople must develop a repeatable plan for getting their sales conversations started, even if they are pitching an audience of one. Below are four simple questions that may be weaved into any casual interaction to help develop a meaningful conversation:

1. What are you doing or working on now?

2. What do you like about what you are doing now?

3. What do you dislike about what you are doing now?

4. What would you like to change?

The reason that these questions consistently work is that they effectively and quickly cover the bulk of the subject matter you need to understand. You may phrase them any number of ways and put your own unique spin on the delivery, but remember to cover the key points: *Now, Like, Dislike and Change*. Through practicing this exercise, you are gaining valuable insights into your prospect's business. This works repeatedly and well because as I like to remind salespeople:

No one cares how much you know until they
know how much you care about them.

When you pose these four questions to your prospect, you are displaying genuine interest in him or her as well as starting a dialogue. Most likely, a quality conversation between the two of you will ensue, instead of a one-sided hurried pitch about your product or service that carries no guarantee of generating interest from your prospect.

The Spin

Even the most novice sales professionals know that asking questions to uncover opportunities is an important aspect of their job. The Business section at most bookstores is filled with advice geared toward training you on how and when to ask the *right* questions. *SPIN Selling* by Neil Rackham, one of the best-selling business books of all time, is one of my personal favorites. As you might realize by this point in my book, I have an affinity for easy-to-remember acronyms, of which SPIN is one of the best. Each letter of SPIN represents a different type of question that when answered by your prospect, will reveal information relevant to a potential purchase.

S - Situational Questions ask the prospect for basic data and background, essentially framing the current "situation" faced by your prospect.

P - **Problem Questions** explore challenges or difficulties that your prospect might want to fix.

I - **Implication Questions** explore the effects of a solution, or in some cases, the effects that might arise if a current problem is not solved. (As the book sets forth, these are among the most powerful questions)

N - **Needs/Payoff Questions** are those that get the customer to actually relay to you the benefit of the solution or tell you why he or she should buy your product.

I cannot speak highly enough about SPIN selling and have recommended the book to all of my sales teams. However, although SPIN selling appears to be a fairly uncomplicated process, I have found that many salespeople have had a difficult time remembering when to put the process into practice. That is the main reason for why I recommend using the four questions to quickly create the "right" conversation.

Take ACT-ion

Here is this Act's ACT-ion: On your next sales call, be prepared to start the conversation and do it by asking the four simple questions. Watch how quickly your targeted prospect engages and listen to how much he or she is willing to divulge as a result of expending a minimal amount of effort. Genius? Surely not. Complicated? Not at all. Memorize the questions; remember to cover *Now, Like, Dislike and Change*; and give the technique a try. Once you learn that you can make more money by simply having a quality conversation, you will never again choose to make a conventional presentation.

Act 20

Building a Repeatable Process

Pick a sport - one that you play frequently and really enjoy. Golf? Tennis? Skiing? Whatever it is, I'm sure you'll agree that on some days you play very well while on other days, your performance is lacking. As amateur athletes, we all enjoy the games we play, but let's be honest - most of us are often making it up as we go along. Professional athletes on the other hand, treat their sport as an exact science and always practice to perfect their performance. They know that only by mastering repeatable processes will they be able to perform at the highest level when the pressure is on or when the competition gets particularly tough.

Actors represent another example of professionals who rely on repeated processes for their success. On stage or on screen, all actors work from scripts, but rarely sound as if they are reading from one. They have rehearsed their lines so many times that their delivery sounds completely natural. Even comic actors, who are applauded for their ability to improvise, use scripts and know exactly where their stories are heading. And the best improvised lines - the ones that get the most laughs - invariably end up being added into the script for repeated use in the future.

Like athletes and actors, salespeople can only ensure consistent performance in the field by developing repeatable scripts and mastering their delivery. Since we often get only one chance to impress our prospects, carefully written and well-rehearsed sales talks are must-haves. And we owe it to our audience - comprised of shareholders, family members, and anyone else who might be counting on us to close business - to perform flawlessly under pressure.

I have found that writing a sales script may be both challenging and enjoyable, since we have an opportunity to use our own words and craft it in our own style. The same way that you would find it thrilling to use your own style to "stick the landing" on an epic ski jump, you would be equally excited about closing a deal with your own unique script. Of course, no repeatable process will work every time, but perfection is not what we're seeking in sales. We simply want to win a lot more than we lose.

Rarely have I met a salesperson who uses a consistent opening line on every sales call. Even successful salespeople use random "shoot from the hip" dialogue. Some people open their tablet devices, while others dive right into a digital presentation without even setting up their pitch with a series of questions. As a result, prospects often take control of the conversation by firing questions out of the gate. You can see this happen to you simply by counting the questions you've been asked. Answer three questions in row, without asking one on your own, and you'll quickly realize you've completely lost control of the sales conversation.

In order for you to take command of your meetings and to control the quality of your conversations, you must be prepared. Just as an actor shows up for the shoot, knowing their lines, I always recommend that having a script committed to memory will make your calls easier and most of all repeatedly successful. By memorized, I mean that you can deliver it naturally and flawlessly in one take with cameras metaphorically rolling. Your actions will set the agenda, establish the tone of the discussion, create a timeframe, and secure an agreement from the prospect to move forward. A solid repeatable process won't necessarily guarantee that you get the sale, but putting it into practice will give you the best chance to win in a far greater percentage of the time.

Take ACT-ion

Here is this Act's ACT-ion: What are three things that you want to accomplish with every prospect? Write them down and then create your own repeatable, compelling, odds-enhancing script. Here's a basic wireframe to help you get started:

"Mr. Owner, thank you for having me here. I know you're busy, so I'll be brief. Essentially there are three things I would like to do today. First I would like to...

(Perhaps introduce yourself and your company.)

"Then I would like for you to..."

(What do you want Mr. Owner to do? If you say, "Buy now," then you are not appealing to their WIIFM - What's In It For Me. Buying something now is only what's in it for you. Remember that this is a first date, so be careful with what you request. You might try asking about the business, so you can discover: what your prospect is doing now, what they like and dislike, and what they would like to change. Learn about your prospect before going further.)

"Finally, if we find a potential fit for both of us, I would like for us to..."

(Get married? Have a baby? Not on the first date! What next steps would you like to accomplish to move Mr. Owner up the Sales Decision Chain?)

"I asked for a half hour, but we could do all of this in fifteen minutes, unless you have questions. Does that sound fair?"

Once you have your script, memorize it like an actor would. Read the first line, look away, say it out loud and repeat it until you get it just right. Now read the second line, look away and say both lines out loud until you nail them. Keep going until you can deliver the entire script effortlessly.

If you were auditioning for an A-List movie which would give you the opportunity to work opposite your favorite actor, you would need to absolutely know your lines to convince the casting director that you were ready for the role. Treat your sales appointments with key decision makers like once-in-a-lifetime auditions and if you want to close the deal, you must be prepared to get the part of the winning provider of whatever it is you may be selling.

Act 21

Handling Objections
with Feel, Felt, Found

Objections seem to arise at the worst times - usually when you're close to finalizing a deal. Listening to them being voiced by a prospect may be frustrating, and some sales people think it also may use up valuable time and slow down the sales process. But objections do not have to block your progress.

One of the best ways to gently shift your customers into a new way of thinking is to employ a well-known strategy called "feel, felt, found." Here's a short script that demonstrates how it works:

*"Salespeople hate hidden objections. Wow, do I understand how you **feel**. It used to drive me nuts when prospects didn't buy and never told me why they opted out. Nobody has **felt** this more than me. However, I **found** that by simply asking if there*

were anything I was missing, I could draw out our prospect's
objections with no fear of losing the deal."

It turns out that empathy is a powerful ally when it comes
to selling. Letting prospects know that you once **felt** the same
way as they have felt in certain situations, establishes a level
of harmony. This level of harmony helps to open the door to
overcoming the objection, by letting your prospect know that
not only is okay for them to voice their objections, but at one
time, you may have a shared the very same opinion. You will
find that if you are empathetic with your prospects opinion or
position, there will be more of an opportunity to steer them
down an alternative path that might lead more quickly to a
final transaction. To help me remember this important technique, I wrote the following in my sales notes many years ago:

"Remember how good it feels to feel felt."

Think about that phrase for a moment. When it seems
that no one but you could understand your predicament,
how good does it feel when you meet someone who truly
empathizes with your situation? How much better does it feel
when you encounter a person who agrees with your position
and perhaps has even shared a similar experience? How great
does it feel when the person acknowledges that he or she
completely understands from where you're coming? These are
the people with whom you should be more than happy to be
around, especially during difficult times. Don't we all want to

spend time with people that "get" us?

In business, when your customers know that you have **felt** the same way, you will **find** them to be more cooperative, often to the point that they will often bend over backwards to support your cause, simply because you have empathized with theirs. There are many ways to use "feel, felt, found" and whether you are new to the technique or an old pro, these words will lead you to greater success. By incorporating them into your sales scripts, you will be able to frequently defeat common objections. But your best results will be assured when you have mastered a second communication-improving technique called "clearing up the ambiguity."

Clearing Up the Ambiguity

Have you ever had to await a final decision from "the board" or "the powers that be?" Have you ever heard your prospect say, "I need to see what *they* want to do?" How about when someone has said that he or she had "a ton to do" before he or she could make a decision? All of these phrases are used unconsciously, while at the same time, quite deliberately by prospects to create ambiguity in order to slow down the need for a final decision. Even so, business ambiguity represents nothing more than simple, common objections.

My least favorite ambiguous term of them all is the word "they." Who exactly are "they?" When you hear your prospect say that a third party will be influencing the decision, you must find out who "they" are. After all, it's going to be very difficult to influence "them" if you have never met them. My second least favorite ambiguous term is "a long time." If something is said to take a "long time," it's important to get a better definition of how long are we talking about. If you're waiting for a train, two hours really is a "long time," but if you're waiting for contract to come back from the attorney's office, thirty days or more may be more than reasonable.

A rep with whom I once traveled finished an outstanding sales call with a quality prospect, and to his frustration, was told by the prospect that she would "see what he wants to do." Wisely, the rep asked who "he" was. By attempting to clear up the ambiguity, we learned that "he" was the prospect's boss and that he kept an office in the neighboring city, which ironically, was the next stop on our travel cloverleaf.

The information that we had learned enabled us to set up a lunch appointment with the boss, that very same day. We also told our prospect that as a favor to her, we would personally deliver the document to her boss and obtain the required signature. Since we had succeeded in clearing up the ambiguity, we were rewarded with a signed contract by that afternoon. That scenario describes what I call "speeding up the sales process" and it never would have occurred had the rep not cleared up the ambiguous term "he" the moment he heard it.

Exposing Hidden Objections

Using "feel, felt, found" not only helps to clear up the ambiguity, it also exposes what are often referred to as hidden objections. Personally, I don't believe that there are hidden objections since a properly executed sales conversation would not leave any objection uncovered. But hidden objections aren't really the problem. The problem is that salespeople are all too willing to accept ambiguity for fear that real objections will emerge and kill the deal.

This strategy amounts to taking what you can get and hoping for the best, or what I like to call "spray and pray" selling. Spraying a pile of brochures on the table and praying that a prospect will find something he or she wants does not constitute quality selling. If you want to be considered an outstanding salesperson, you must refuse to accept ambiguity and become a pro at using "feel, felt, found" to overcome objections.

Take ACT-ion

Here is this Act's ACT-ion: Write down the three most common objections you usually hear from your prospects. What are they? Is price an issue? Shipping charges? The competition? Write each of them down to acknowledge that you know exactly what's coming on your next sales call. Next, build your repeatable script using the "feel, felt, found" technique so that you are prepared to overcome each of the identified objections. Finally, practice to make perfect, and get ready to watch the most common objections disappear – almost as quickly as they are voiced.

Act 22

Making "No" Okay

We have spent a fair amount of time talking about the word "no" and the role it plays in winning and losing sales. You have already learned that "no" is not a deal killer, but let's take it one step further and make it the response you *want* to hear from your prospects. In this Act, I will introduce a subtle, yet effective technique I call "making no okay" that really does speed up the decision process.

Since buyers are risk averse by their very nature, "making no okay" involves a slight twist on reverse psychology, i.e. how to effectively pull prospects into your way of thinking by taking an opportunity away from them rather than pushing your products forward. In order for this technique to work, two people (one of whom is you) must be okay with receiving a final answer of "no." Winning still remains the objective, but in order to win, you must be willing to lose. If you're not willing to lose, the angst associated with the need to make the sale will be evident and ruin your chances of getting the "yes" that you desire. You must be content with putting a "yes" in the bank or even okay with not finishing first for this tactic to work effectively. Here's a simple script for your consideration:

"Mr. Owner, I can see that you have some concerns and I want you to know that I'm okay with that. I would not want you to move forward with this product unless you felt 100 percent certain that it would be effective in your business and that our plan would result in a solid return on your investment. Before we proceed, could you promise me that you are certain of these two things?"

There are a couple of reasons that this approach works. First, if you sell something that dies a dusty death in the drawer, you are negatively impacting your future in the market. It must be personally important that you sell your product the right way, to the right people, for the right customers and in a way that leaves your buyer pleased with his or her purchase.

In order to get the behavioral change we need from our prospects, particularly in Steps 4-7 of the Sales Decision Chain (where prospects go from **willing to do** to **telling everyone else what they are doing**), attaining customer satisfaction is crucial. Becoming proficient at guiding prospects through these steps is the key to making more money in your market. Making "no" okay is most effective at points that are later in the Sales Decision Chain.

4. From **willing to do** to **doing**

5. From **doing** to **glad they did**

6. From **glad they did** to **continuing to do**

7. And finally, to **telling everyone else what they are doing**!

By relaying to your prospect that you need to know that he or she is confident in his or her purchase, you have taken the most important step toward achieving referral-level customer satisfaction. Your future sales will be impacted by the quality of your execution both at the point of sale *and* during the installation process.

The second reason why this technique works is that it effectively contradicts the common perception of salespeople as pushers. By letting your prospects know that you want them to be confident with their decision, you become a puller, drawing them to you by being sincere, open, and brave enough to allow a risk-averse person to make a decision in his or her own timeframe. Most prospects will move swiftly toward making a decision if they are given time to process matters on their own time, rather than being hurried or pressed by a pusher. Have you ever been "pushed" right off the floor of a retail store by a salesperson who insists on "helping" you? That person was most likely thinking *only* about his or her commission, and not necessarily your satisfaction, when they behave overly helpful.

Take ACT-ion

This Act contains two ACT-ions. Here is your first: Create a short list of prospects whom you might have pressured over the last few months and call each of them to just check in. Expect that as on previous calls, you will probably get a "no," but this time tell your prospects that "no is okay." In reality, you will have just put a "yes" in the bank that may be withdrawn once your product gains further traction in the market.

Your second ACT-ion is to identify a customer to whom you have previously sold who might not be using your product or service. Put on your shoes, go visit him or her and be ready to refund the sale, if necessary. In other words, go undo a done deal and do it with a smile. I realize we're not in the business of giving out refunds, but if you really want your territory to thrive, you can't afford to have even a single product sitting in the drawer collecting dust.

Undoing a done deal will have a profound two-fold effect. First, by allowing a customer to back out of a decision that he or she might have regretted, you will have created a lifelong ally. Second, by showing that you are willing to lose a deal, your customer might actually apologize and begin to use your product or service once again. In either case, you win and word-of-mouth endorsements are sure to follow.

Act 23

Speaking from Experience

How many times have you heard the phrase, "that will never work," particularly from someone who has had no basis to support the claim? As a sales manager, I have heard it often and know that a healthy debate will typically follow. Unfortunately, many salespeople cave too early to objections like these, usually because they lack enough personal experience with the product or service and are unable to convince their prospect that it *will* work.

For example, if you're selling oysters and have never tried them because you think they look disgusting, you will be in trouble when your prospect asks you how they taste. Only by trying the oysters will you be able to gain the insight you need to sell the entire shipment. And even if you don't like them, you could close the sale by speaking from experience and relying on testimonials from your customers who do like oysters.

Even the most combative objectors will lose the debate if they answer, "no" to the question, "have you tried it?" If an answer is to be credible, there needs to be some level of knowledge of the subject matter. An opinion, particularly your uniformed one, would not likely carry much weight.

A Mountain of Experience

A few years ago, I was at dinner with a group of colleagues, and the subject of mountain climbing came up. One person expressed the opinion that climbing Mount Kilimanjaro couldn't be that difficult, given the number of seemingly average athletes who have made it to the top.

"Not hard?" I asked. "C'mon, that must be incredibly hard to achieve. I mean, "Kill-a-Man" is right there in the name."

"I disagree. It's can't be that tough," my friend insisted.

It was at that point that a third person at the table asked if either of us had ever been to or climbed Mount Kilimanjaro. Our answer, which we actually stated simultaneously, was "no."

Our female colleague pointed out that both of us were merely expressing opinions and began to tell us about *her* climb to that very summit the previous year. According to her, the climb was exceedingly difficult and required three grueling days to reach the summit. She told us that along the way, she had to pass through five climate zones including temperatures that dropped well below zero degrees. And then of course, she needed to come back down! She also told us that she is convinced that the only reason she "made it" up and back was that she had trained intensely for six months in order to be fit enough for the feat.

It still strikes me as rather funny that the one person who could actually speak from personal experience appropriately put two armchair mountain climbers in their places. And because she could speak from experience, she was the one who controlled the direction of the conversation. If the three of us had been at dinner with a prospect who wanted to purchase an African mountain climbing expedition, I'm certain that my female colleague would have been the only one to have made the sale.

Take ACT-ion

Here's this Act's ACT-ion: Since we now know the importance of speaking from experience, think about your own experiences with the products or services you are selling. Have you tried them? Do they work? Would you spend your hard earned money on them if you were in your prospect's shoes? Next, write down your stories of personal experiences with the products or services you are selling and imagine how you might use them to overcome objections in your sales conversations.

If you receive an objection related to why it "won't work," your customer's experience will you explain in detail why you know that it absolutely will.

Act 24

Let's Do This

Few people will decline buying a product or service that has been proven to have improved a process or saved money, especially if the risk to them is minimal. A line that helps to get prospects to commit is, "Let's do this..." followed by a risk-free, or at minimum, a risk-reducing proposition. This technique relies on the premise that nothing you sell is permanent unless the customer is completely satisfied. The more effectively you are able to convey this point, the more willing your prospects will be to try something new, if only to gain some experience with your product or service.

Friends and customers like to needle me about my frequent use of "let's do this." When that happens, I always get a good chuckle since they don't seem to realize that while they are teasing me, we are often doing exactly what I had suggested, by my use of "let's do this..." in the first place. Similarly, employing this tactic while selling will result in getting your prospects to follow your lead. Let's take a look at how this works.

When shopping at a clothing store, you may try on a piece of clothing if you're unsure about whether or not to purchase it. In fact, any good retailer would probably suggest that you do just that. Even if after trying on the item, and you are still undecided about buying it, you may buy it with the option of being able to return it. Retailers know that once we have a product in our possession, we have made a psychological commitment to it, which in turn has increased the likelihood that we will keep it. Think about how many times this practice has turned your "maybe" into a "yes." Furthermore, think about how many times you have gone to return a previously purchased item only to leave the store with something else. Retailers also know that once you have made an initial purchase, you're unlikely to leave their store empty-handed.

Another technique utilized by warehouse retail giants is to offer free samples in the store. These companies know that they will sell more boxes of any food item for example, if they could get customers to take just one small bite. Talk about reducing a buyer's risk; if the food tastes good, a purchase makes sense. This practice will work in your business, too. When your sale is stuck in neutral, "let's do this" gives you the ability to offer your prospect a trial period that will get the sales process back into gear.

Take ACT-ion

So here is this Act's ACT-ion: Let's do this...write down the name of a prospect whom you have been trying to close, but with whom the sales process has come to a virtual standstill. Who is your slow moving target? Refer to the Sales Decision Chain and know that the slow movers usually get stuck on Step 3 (from **considering** to **willing to do**) and Step 4 (from **willing to do** to **doing**). They're likely moving slowly or nervous about making a decision because they need more information or are afraid that your proposal might not work.

To move them along, think about how you could reframe your offer to reduce their risk and in turn, their fear of engaging. Create a risk-free pilot program, which your prospect cannot refuse, write it down, and have it ready to deliver the next time you meet. With proper execution, you will elicit a considerably more positive response that will allow you to lead them down the path to a sale.

Act 25

Hooks, Lines, and Selling with Stories

"Big wheels keep on turning. Carry me home to see my kin. Singing songs about the Southland. I miss Alabamy once again. And I think it's a sin. Yes I do."

The iconic hit song, *Sweet Home Alabama*, was made famous by the band Lynyrd Skynyrd. Who could forget the memorable guitar riff that starts the song, and perhaps, the even more brilliant suggestion by guitarist Ronnie Van Zant to "turn it up" right before the first verse? What many people don't realize is that Van Zant's suggested line was never supposed to make it into the final cut of the song. Apparently, he had been simply asking the engineer to turn up his headphones. But the producer liked the line so much that he kept it. And with that, Rock 'n' Roll history was made.

I share this story to demonstrate the importance of having a hook - a great line - followed by a verifiable short story to illustrate your point. If you think that making your case in only a few minutes in front of your prospect is difficult, imagine the obstacles faced by a songwriter. Songwriters have just eight seconds to command a listener's attention or "make their sale," to ensure that the listener sticks around for the rest of the song. Eight seconds is the average amount of time it takes for people to change the station or skip to the next track if they don't like what they have heard. Imagine - just eight seconds – which is the reason why songwriters work so hard on creating a great hook.

A "hook" in sales is something you could say over and over again and will always grab your prospect's attention. A "line" is best described as a statement with which most prospects will agree. Delivered effectively, the right hook and line will put you in a position to share a true story, which like a great song, should command a thorough listening. Think about this the next time you listen to *Sweet Home Alabama*. Most listeners get hooked on the guitar riff; often comply with the line "turn it up;" and finally, listen to the entire song.

After delivering your hook and line, you must tell a story that is simple and always features good news or new information that keeps your prospect's attention. For example, using subtle, intellectual flattery such as "I'm sure you know that the line 'turn it up' in *Sweet Home Alabama* was a happy accident" will prove far more effective than wagering, "I'll bet you didn't know..." It is irrelevant whether your prospect actually knew the fact of which you had just spoken. By *assuming* that he or she knew, you have given him or her the respect needed to keep him or her engaged.

Creating Your Hook, Line and Story

Like the band Lynyrd Skynyrd, your company might also have a 1 hit on its hands with its product or service. But in order for you to sell that product or service, you must have a few good hooks, lines and stories. Here is an example of a hook, line and story that I had prepared for a client who was in the medical device industry.

The Hook

"Dr. Jones, have you ever seen one of these? This revolutionary device puts the power of cold in the palm of your hand and delivers immediate temporary pain relief for patients with symptoms of chronic knee pain."

The Line with Which Most Doctors Will Agree

"I'm sure you're aware that adverse systemic side effects from many drugs and injected agents are costing our health system over $100 billion dollars annually. I'm sure you're also aware that many patients complain that many common drugs don't even stop the localized pain."

The Short Story

*"Here's a cool story, pun intended, that shows just how well
this device works. A few weeks ago, I was with Dr. Jackson
in New York and we treated a sixty-one-year-old man
who had given up golf due to an arthritic condition that
was causing debilitating pain in his knee. Honestly, he
could barely walk. We arranged to meet him prior to his
second treatment, and we brought along our device."*

*"When I asked him how the first treatment had gone, he
offered effusive praise, stating that he hadn't experienced
pain for more than five months until just one week ago, when
the treatment wore off. He also said that he had begun
playing golf again only one day after the treatment."*

*"Dr. Jones, we don't have anyone in your area who is using
the device and that's why I wanted to show it to you today.
I could have you speak with Dr. Jackson if you would
like, but you should really speak with this patient."*

Take ACT-ion

Here is this Act's ACT-ion: First, think carefully about the
product or service you are selling and come up with a hook
or short sentence that will really grab your prospect's attention. You should be able to recite it in ten seconds or less.
Next, write down a line or statement with which most of your

prospects would agree. If you sell hotel rooms for example, most hotel owners would surely agree that last-minute cancellations are the bane of their existence. Your statement should show your prospect that you understand or empathize with his or her position. Finally, write out a short story that relays a previous success with another customer. Similar to the words of one of your favorite songs, your hook, line, and short story should be easy to remember so they may be used again and again to gain listeners' attention and generate more opportunities to win.

Act 26

Showing Up and Doing Your Job

You have probably heard that "90 percent of sales are made by just showing up." And I'm sure that you, like 90 percent of salespeople, would say that you show up most of the time. Let's face it - showing up *all of the time* is not easy to do. In fact, when faced with a sales opportunity, only 10 percent of all salespeople cast excuses aside and find a way to show up *every time.* But here's what's really interesting: 90 percent of all sales are made by 10 percent of all salespeople. Care to know who the 10 percent might be?

If you want to increase your sales numbers and be a consistent winner, you must find a way to be in the 10 percent of all salespeople who make 90 percent of all sales. Or in other words, you must ensure that you are never passing up an opportunity to see a prospect or customer in person.

- Showing up sends a clear message that you are the one salesperson who cares the most about your prospect or customer.

- Showing up ensures that you will always be part of the sales conversation.

- Showing up means that you want the sale more than anyone else.

- The more often you show up, the more products you will sell.

There are a number of ways to show up, but here's the easiest one: Call or follow up your leads the moment you receive them. That sounds simple enough, but if it's so easy, why do few salespeople actually do this? They go to other meetings first, wait until they get home or wait for their designated day to go into the office, which usually occurs at the end of the week. Unfortunately for them, "time kills deals." Need proof? Call a contractor about a problem in your house. A contractor is in sales, right? You would think that he or she would need the business. But how long does it usually take to hear back from the contractor after you have left your message?

And what was the slow responder's excuse for the delayed response? Most of the time, the contractor will tell you that he or she was too busy. Too busy to discuss new business? Why would anyone want to buy from that contractor again? If your goal is to sell more goods and services, there is no valid excuse for a delayed response to an incoming lead. Even if you truly could not speak at the moment, it's easy to make a call, if only to schedule a future time to talk. The fact that you at least acknowledged the call will speak volumes about your desire to serve your customers.

Only One Can be Number One

Granted, it's not always easy to see more people in person or to be this fast in responding to leads. Using a football analogy, it's no easier for a quarterback to go over the game plan "one more time" prior to kickoff. But you know that the New England Patriot's Tom Brady makes the time to do just that. Sure, all quarterbacks are highly competitive, but Tom Brady seems to want to win more than anyone else and does whatever it takes to ensure that his team comes out on top. Some people have contended that he is the best quarterback in the history of football. I believe that two of the reasons Brady has multiple championship rings are that he *always* shows up and is *always* fully prepared to face each opponent.

Speaking of the New England Patriots, you might have read about the small sign in their locker room, mounted conspicuously next to the door leading out to the field. It contains just three extremely powerful words:

DO YOUR JOB

Do you think this phrase provides the Patriots' players with the inspiration they need to psych out the competition? You bet it does! This sign serves as a constant reminder to team members each and every time they enter or exit the locker room, that in order to succeed, they must be better than the rest - even if only by the slimmest of margins.

Take ACT-ion

Here is this Act's ACT-ion, one that will help you show up more often and gain an edge over the competition: Make your own "DO YOUR JOB" sign and post it in your office, in a place where you will see it each and every day. Does this sound silly or seem like a waste of time? Remember that it doesn't to New England Patriot's Head Coach, Bill Belichik. He put this phrase next to the locker room entrance because he knows that when it comes to gaining an advantage over the competition, the small stuff really matters. And so should you.

Act 27

Avoiding Dead Air

Since you have already learned that a presentation is really just a conversation, the only way to properly conclude it is with an open discussion from all participants. Most salespeople would agree with this statement, but they would also agree that when they conclude by asking their prospects, "Are there any questions?" a discussion often doesn't follow. Instead, they get "dead air," a time period during which no one – not the salesperson or their prospects – seems to have anything to say.

In radio and television broadcasting, "dead air" refers to a time period when the program material comes to an unexpected halt. Broadcast teams work hard to prevent it from happening, in large part because they know that if it occurs during commercial breaks, it could cost their networks considerable advertising revenue. Similarly, salespeople must work hard to avoid "dead air" at the conclusion of a presentation or it could cost them a deal. So how is this best accomplished?

A Better Manner of Closing

I like to remind myself that Abraham Lincoln did not have access to digital technologies, those which today, are commonly used by salespeople to enhance presentations and to help gain and keep the attention of their audiences. In 1863, President Lincoln only had a pen (a quill actually) and paper, yet he made one of the greatest presentations of all time when he delivered the *Gettysburg Address*. I share the full content of the speech as a reminder that keeping it simple never goes out of style:

"Fourscore and seven years ago our fathers brought forth on this continent a new nation, conceived in Liberty, and dedicated to the proposition that all men are created equal.

Now we are engaged in a great civil war, testing whether that nation, or any nation so conceived and so dedicated, can long endure. We are met on a great battlefield of that war. We have come to dedicate a portion of that field as a final resting place for those who here gave their lives that that nation might live. It is altogether fitting and proper that we should do this.

But, in a larger sense, we cannot dedicate - we cannot consecrate - we cannot hallow - this ground. The brave men, living and dead, who struggled here, have consecrated it, far above our poor power to add or detract. The world will little note nor long remember what we say here, but it can never forget what they did here. It is for us the living, rather, to be dedicated here to the unfinished work which they who fought here have thus far so nobly advanced. It is rather for us to be here dedicated to the great task remaining before us - that from these honored dead we take increased devotion to that cause for which they gave the last full measure of devotion; that we here highly resolve that these dead shall not have died in vain; that this nation, under God, shall have a new birth of freedom; and that government of the people, by the people, for the people, shall not perish from the earth."

- Abraham Lincoln, November 19, 1863

It's fairly safe to assume that after President Lincoln was done delivering this speech, he did not present a white space-laden slide that said "Thank you," "The End," or worse yet, "Questions?" And it's doubtful that anyone in the audience asked, "May I get a soft copy of the speech?" But we all know that Lincoln's message would resonate for the ages.

A sales presentation should have a similar non-awkward conclusion. Instead of closing by asking, "Are there any questions?" when there might be none, ask the following:

"If there are no questions, then I have one for you. What do you think about what I just said?"

This manner of closing suggests that your time with your audience was not intended to simply share and then awkwardly stall, but was intended to move them up the Sales Decision

Chain. By asking your prospects what they think and even calling on someone to respond, you are encouraging them to share their opinions and reveal any objections that otherwise might have been missed.

Dismissing Yourself

Another piece of worthwhile advice for helping close your presentation is to never overstay your welcome. When you're finished with your presentation or conversation, regardless of how much time might be left, do the opposite of what most salespeople do and end your presentation early.

"You know, that's a great point you make, but I have only scheduled an hour today. In order to be respectful of your time and to stay on schedule with the rest of my day, I really have to go. Perhaps we could schedule another time to meet."

By dismissing yourself prior to the end of your designated timeframe, you are taking control of the next steps of the Sales Decision Chain. You have successfully engaged your prospect and piqued his or her interest, and now most importantly, you have encouraged your prospect to initiate further discussion. In other words, you have created a page-turning event, leaving your audience wanting more.

Take ACT-ion

Here is this Act's ACT-ion: Select a prospect with whom you are working, decide where he or she is in the Sales Decision Chain and before your next call, write down the *reasonable* minimum next action you would like him or her to take. It is reasonable for your prospect to want to speak with others who are successfully using your products. But it is *unreasonable* for you to ask him or her to drop all currently installed, competitive products and to immediately switch to yours.

Next, create a presentation that will help to achieve the goal of getting the prospect to take that minimum next action, and then play it out in your head, considering all possible outcomes. If your prospect agrees to the next step, your work is done and this is the time to dismiss yourself in order to avoid dead air. If your prospect has still not arrived at your intended destination, asking for feedback about the information provided will reveal the objections and allow you to convince him or her that the next step would be in his or her best interest.

Part Five

Knowing Thyself

The final part of our journey explores the various roles that exist in a sales organization, in order to help you determine if your current role is in alignment with your strengths or whether a different role might lead to greater success. Sadly, many people never find their "true love" in business because they lack an understanding of their personal strengths and therefore fail to maximize their opportunities. From the remaining pages ahead, my hope is that you will learn today "who you are," and as a result, find greater happiness in both business and in life.

Act 28

Discovering Your Ideal Role

The final part of this book is designed to help you discover your ideal role in the world of sales, since knowing thyself is invaluable as it relates to achieving and exceeding your potential. In a nutshell, if you're a dog, you should work hard to be the best dog that you could be. You should run fast, bark confidently, do whatever it takes to win more treats and wag your tail while you're enjoying them. There would be no greater waste of time than if you tried to be a cat, because you are a dog. And if someone told you to try being a cat for a while, you would quickly discover that hanging out on a window ledge would not work for you. You are a dog and you belong in the dog park, doing what dogs do best.

No business may survive without a host of team members, all of whom play an important role in fulfilling the company's potential. There are some commonly known terms to categorize the types of salespeople every organization needs in order to thrive: Hunters, Farmers, Coaches, Individual Contributors and Team Players. Determining which category best suits your personality is the key to enjoying a more successful and satisfying sales career.

Assess Your Personality

A popular test used by many companies to help determine in which area people might be best suited is the MBTI (Myers-Briggs Type Indicator) Assessment. This psychometric personality test, dating back to 1921, puts forth a series of behavioral questions to determine a person's individual preference in each of four pairs of personality indicators.

E-Extraversion	or	**I**-Introversion
S-Sensing	or	**N**-Intuition
T-Thinking	or	**F**-Feeling
J-Judging	or	**P**-Perception

When I took the test, I learned that my dominant personality traits are **ENTJ**. E means that I focus more on people and things than ideas. N means that I am more abstract in thinking and prefer to look past experiences like sight, sound, taste, touch and smell. T means that my judgment is ruled by logic, and not by emotion. Finally, J means that I'm more methodical and results-oriented when it comes to getting things done. While many who take the test might ignore the results, I have used mine throughout my career to help determine what type of job would suit me best as well as offer me the quickest path to success.

Maybe you have taken the test yourself. If you haven't, I highly recommend that you take the time to do it. Either way, most of us have a fairly good understanding of who we are. Unfortunately, few of us have used this information to find a suitable career opportunity. Most of us have just let our jobs happen *to* us, instead of making them happen *for* us. In order to help you determine your ideal role in sales, let's look at what it means to be a Hunter, Farmer, Coach, Individual Contributor and Team Player.

Hunters

Hunters are considered to be the cold callers of the sales world and thrive on what *might* happen. For them, it's all about the act of hunting for new business. They enjoy both the exploration as well as the trophies they may receive from closing deals. But these hunters also know that anything worth achieving takes effort. Preparation and hard work are the hallmarks of the hunter.

In actuality, hunters are the best prepared of all salespeople. Before venturing into the woods, good hunters know specifically where they want to go; what route they're going to take to get there; where they're going to stop along the way; and what they're going to do at each juncture. Hunters know that a precise plan of action will provide them with the greatest odds of achieving success. Successful hunters are also masters at identifying the most desirable targets and then positioning themselves to make the very best shot. Sometimes, one shot is all that it takes, but missing the mark the first time is of no concern to expert hunters. They will return to the same place the next week, perhaps with a different strategy in mind, and with the expectation of a different outcome.

Each day, the hunter asks, "Is today the day I'm going to close the biggest deal of my life?" And the hunter also provides the answer: "Maybe so, but I'll never know unless I go out and look for it." Any organization must hire at least a few solid hunters and compensate them appropriately, if they have expectations to grow their business.

Farmers

If any sales organization is going to succeed, it also needs to employ farmers. Without them, the other employees in the organization would likely go hungry. Farmers have a defined territory or field in which they plant seeds, and are considered to be the experts at caring for those seeds. Farmers enjoy tending to the garden and always strive to make it as bountiful as possible. In sales, farmers are the cultivators of business and succeed by maintaining and growing relationships that have already been established.

Although farmers work with many customers, they often perform their best work alone, rather than working with a team. This allows them to be free from distraction and to focus on being as productive as possible. Independence, personal drive and strategic focus on developing business relationships are the farmer's keys to success.

Coaches

Coaches exist to help players fulfill their potential so that the team may achieve victory after victory. A key personality trait of successful coaches is that they have the hearts of teachers and care deeply for others. Unlike hunters and farmers, coaches remain largely out of view and feel like winners when others around them win. Coaches also know that they gain power and influence by having the confidence to freely give away power and influence. If the team wins, the coach is the first person to give the players all of the credit. But if the team loses, the coach is the first person to accept responsibility for his or her lack of strategic execution.

Sadly, many newly promoted managers don't realize that coaching is a vital part of their role. In baseball, sometimes "go, go, go" is all a runner needs to hear from a coach in order to reach home plate safely. To score more runs, most good salespeople need training, help in developing new ideas and support whenever necessary. An exceptional manager is an effective coach - not a supervisor or a boss.

Individual Contributors

Individual contributors play one of the most important

roles in any organization. Without these focused individuals who regularly contribute new and recurring cash flow to the business through their selling efforts, most companies would fail. Individual contributors may be hunters, farmers, or some combination of these roles, and most are members of a team rather than people who would be responsible for operating a team. Successful individual contributors are self-starters who can effectively manage their time with limited supervision. They fully embrace technology, best evidenced by making regular updates to their CRM, consistently finish what they start, and generally take personal accountability for the tasks that have been assigned to them.

My favorite individual contributor of all time is Batman. Whom did the Police Chief call when Gotham City had a real problem? He called Batman. However, when something went wrong, the pressure was also on Batman to fix it. Similarly in sales, when business is down, much of the blame is placed on individual contributors, usually by people who wouldn't even be able to get the Batmobile out of the garage. Like Batman, individual contributors are usually resilient to criticism and always seem to find a way to get things back on track.

Team Players

No individual contributor, hunter, or farmer would experience any level of sustained success in sales without being surrounded by great team players - including customer support representatives, manufacturing resources and operational personnel. Teams win when each player on the team performs with the other members' best interests in mind. One of the key traits of good team players is that they have the maturity to be "less about me and more about we." As the acronym for TEAM reminds us: Together Everyone Achieves More.

Still, there are always some people who are better team players than others. A good example of an outstanding team player would be Dwayne Wade of the NBA's Miami Heat. Rather than seeking free agency status to maximize his financial gain, he accepted less than his full market value in each of the three contracts that he signed. As a result of his personal sacrifice to help build a great team, he has been rewarded with three Championship rings.

The Wrong Role

Since the purpose of this Act is to help you discover your ideal sales role, we should discuss how working in the wrong role could negatively impact your career. Here's a story of a salesperson who began his career as an individual contributor; hunted more than his fair share of new business; and farmed his way to acquiring many outstanding customers. But when he was promoted to manager, he became completely ineffective and in fact, became a detriment to the overall success of the company. It turned out that the skills required to succeed in management were vastly different than the skills that had made this salesperson so outstanding in his previous role.

Rick was a good salesperson who cared about his customers, worked hard, showed up every day and performed his job as an individual contributor extremely well. Unfortunately, he had few friends among his co-workers. This was likely due to the fact that nearly every time something good happened as a result of a team effort, Rick would take the credit. Few people thought Rick was suitable for any role other than the one he was in, but he was doing everything possible to earn a promotion. One day, as fate would have it, he was selected to be the manager over a group of former peers.

Rick embraced his new role, but his micromanagement style drained the life out of the members on his team. As a result, the company experienced a nearly 100 percent turnover in his direct reporting sales force, including those who had achieved a long tenure of success prior to his arrival.

As salespeople exited the company, Rick replaced them with passive personalities who would not question his authority or challenge his actions. Like most micromanagers, he closed the door to new approaches or ideas, effectively eliminating the company's selling creativity. The resulting loss of revenue was a direct consequence of a deflated sales culture.

In Rick's defense, he was not entirely responsible for his inability to effectively perform in his new management role. Some of the fault rested with the person who had promoted him into a position that was not aligned with his natural abilities. This "wrong role" caused Rick to adopt an attitude of self-preservation that in turn, had resulted in his abrasive management style.

Who Are You?

As you can see, there is a unique set of personality traits associated with each type of salesperson. If you have no fear of cold calling and would become easily bored seeing the same customers, week in and week out, without the dream of closing a new big deal, you would probably make an outstanding hunter. If you enjoy building relationships with existing customers and like taking clients out to dinner, you would probably be best suited to farming. And so the logic goes...

Take ACT-ion

Here is this Act's ACT-ion: Know thyself. Now that you better understand each of these sales roles, determine which one would be best suited to *your* personality. Properly identifying "who you are" will enable you to maximize your productivity and ultimately, your success. If you discover that you are in the wrong role, now might be the time to consider making a change in order to allow yourself to become the best that you can be.

Act 29

Ready, Set, Sell!

*The same things done the same old way
reveal the same results as yesterday.*

As a person who is a strong and vocal proponent of taking action, I have often repeated the aforementioned statement to salespeople whose numbers are not where they want them to be. We all seem to have an innate desire to cling to what we know and to fear what we do not.

At the beginning of this book, I shared a notion that just one day could make all the difference in your sales performance, and in turn, the amount of money you could earn. If you have completed each Act's ACT-ion, then TODAY is your day to begin to become a better salesperson. What is your next step? Will you choose to do the same things the same way and get the same results as yesterday? Or, will you try something new? If beginning today, you put these tips, techniques and tactics into practice, then the percentage-wise improvement you are seeking will soon follow. And if for any reason, you still find yourself stuck in the sales process with any of your prospects, refer to the only three things that you can control as a salesperson and determine where you could make an improvement.

Your Attitude
The Quantity of Your Sales Calls
The Quality of Your Sales Calls

If you demonstrate to prospects that you care about the sales process as you guide them through every step of the Sales Decision Chain, you and your clients will achieve more success. A friend of mine once told me, "We are not here to see through each other. Instead, we are here to see each other through." I have often repeated that quote to other salespeople, since I have found it to be relevant to both selling and to life.

This quote has also reminded me not to judge my prospects, customers, co-workers, friends and family on whatever they are doing, but to simply "be there" to help them be more successful. By applying your new sales skills; effectively communicating the value of your product or service; and truly caring about the outcome of your actions for all parties, everyone WINS.

Now you are **Ready**. Now you are **Set**. And since nothing happens until somebody sells something, get out and **Sell**!

About The Author

Jim Wrigley is the founder of Market Share Sherpas and a professional sales coach who has conducted face-to-face business in all fifty states and abroad. An expert on guiding businesses on the revenue ascent, he has provided sales results seminars to dozens of companies and hundreds of sales representatives across a variety of industries.

Jim was raised in the coastal, New England village of Rowayton, Connecticut, the son of a Yellow Pages salesman and a dental hygienist. A graduate of the University of Connecticut, Jim divides his time today between Park City, Utah and Nashville, Tennessee.

3 1170 00986 4335

CPSIA information can be obtained at www.ICGtesting.com
Printed in the USA
BVOW06s0125130715

408388BV00010B/145/P